A souvenir guide

Ellen Terry at Smallhythe Place
Kent

Veronica Isaac

National Trust

'The Ideal Pre-Raphaelite'

A foreword by Michael Holroyd

Ellen Terry, age 17.
Photograph taken by Mrs Julia Margaret Cameron.
at Freshwater in 1865.

Born in 1847, the daughter of strolling players, Ellen Terry began her theatre career at the age of nine and was continually travelling the theatre circuits. Hers was a crowded, active life and she was soon recognised as an ideal Pre-Raphaelite. She had the proportions of a goddess, audiences felt, and she possessed a genius for making people feel happy. *The Times* was to call her 'the uncrowned queen of England' and Virginia Woolf speculated on how dramatically the course of British history might have changed had she been on the throne instead of Queen Victoria. She appeared to have the spirit of romance and the secret of eternal youth.

With the famous actor-manager Henry Irving she created a cathedral of the arts at the Lyceum Theatre in London. It was a place of popular entertainment enriching the hopes and dreams of audiences. What Hollywood became in the 20th century, the Lyceum was during the late 19th.

But Ellen Terry's private life was very different from what the public who saw her on stage imagined. She had been the child-bride of 'England's Michelangelo', the artist G. F. Watts, who painted her as Joan of Arc and Shakespeare's Ophelia. But the marriage lasted less than a year, ending in much sexual confusion and unhappiness. She ran away to live with a handsome architect and designer William Godwin. She was passionately in love with him and they had two illegitimate children: Edith (Edy) and Edward.

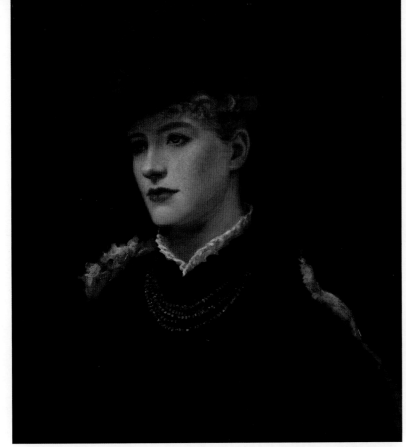

DAME ELLEN TERRY

Opposite This portrait by Julia Margaret Cameron depicts a young Ellen Terry, we think at the time that she was a new bride to G. F. Watts. Though later revised, the image's original title was *Sadness* – perhaps hinting at the unhappy marriage that was to follow?

Above left Ellen Terry in 1876, painted by actor and theatre manager Sir Johnston Forbes-Robertson; oil on canvas

Above right Dame Ellen Terry in 1925

In later life, after William Godwin left her, Ellen seemed unable to stop marrying. But her two later marriages were misadventures while her friendships appeared to be more like love affairs. It was rumoured that she was in love with her friend the playwright Bernard Shaw who had written *Captain Brassbound's Conversion,* his adventurous play, for her.

But the man she really loved was Henry Irving. It was not his great power on stage, which mesmerised his audiences, that attracted her. Nor was it the actor's painted face in their theatre that made him so lovable. It was what he lacked – above all, his terrible loneliness touched her. He had no idea of his beauty. She doted on his looks: his superb brow, the dark eyes and pale skin showing up the hollows of his cheeks.

Ellen's two other loves were her mysterious daughter and mercurial son. She had often been absent from their lives when they were young, putting the theatre first and was frequently away on tours abroad, particularly in America. But she made up for her absence with later possessiveness. Edy was a superb costumier, knitting and needling fiercely like women round the guillotine: 'Edy is enough to make one daft,' Ellen wrote, but she never allowed others to criticise her daughter.

Her son, Edward Gordon, passed most of his life abroad. In 30 years, scattered through five countries, he had 13 children by eight women – one of them the celebrated American dancer Isadora Duncan. But Ellen was rightly proud of his brilliant stage designs and imaginative theories for the theatre.

It is difficult to keep up with Ellen Terry – she was always on the move. By the early 1890s she was living in Winchelsea, East Sussex. One day, when she was out in a pony and trap, she came across a rather dilapidated but picturesque farmhouse set in the water-meadows at Smallhythe in Kent. She took an immediate liking to the place and Irving encouraged her to buy it. But the shepherd who was tenant there did not want to sell it. Some time later, Ellen received a card from him with the words 'House for Sale'. There were two adjacent cottages, a large barn and the Priest House, together with some land. Ellen bought the house and land in 1899 for £1,700 (she purchased the cottages and Priest House later). She was then in her early fifties and would remain there until she died almost 30 years later.

It was a place of repose after her frantic career – pain and anxiety appeared powerless to invade it. Ellen was told that the farmhouse, with its dappled russet roof, had originally been a yeoman's dwelling and was built as the harbour master's headquarters. It was 'a brave old house' with walls of packed timber beams giving on to the green valley and, in the sunshine that radiated them, seeming to reflect something of her naturally happy temperament.

The job of looking after Ellen in old age fell mainly upon her daughter Edy. As her public reputation grew (she was made a Dame of the British Empire in 1925, a few days short of her 80th birthday), so her actual life shrank. She was to die at Smallhythe on 21 July 1928. Her message, 'No funeral gloom, my dears, when I am gone,' was pinned up all round the village. The men wore coloured ties, the women summer dresses, at her funeral. An impromptu guard of honour was formed by the haymakers, shepherds and farmers with their rakes and pitchforks before the church, and inside the congregation sang 'All things bright and beautiful'.

Ellen left Smallhythe to Edy. Edy collected her mother's costumes, including the famous beetle-wing dress she had worn as Lady Macbeth in which John Singer Sargent painted her (a celebrated portrait now in The Tate Britain, London). To these Edy added Henry Irving's stage properties and pictures. Smallhythe is a very personal museum. Visitors can see a painting of Ellen in a play by J. M. Barrie and a decorative poster of Irving by the Beggarstaff Brothers. There are also mementoes of famous actors from a previous generation including David Garrick and Sarah Siddons – as well as a letter from Oscar Wilde. Ellen's bedroom is wonderfully light, a bed made up, a dressing-table prepared for her.

Go into the garden and you are in the very heart of England. Step into the Barn, used for talks and entertainments, and you may feel that Ellen Terry herself could make her entrance any moment.

Michael Holroyd

Far left Smallhythe Place remains a homely and welcoming cottage today

Above left The front door entrance to Smallhythe Place

Below left Ellen as Margaret in the Lyceum production of *Faust* in 1885

Above right Ellen's book of Shakespeare's plays

Ellen Terry: 'A Useful Actress'

Ellen Terry was immersed in the world of the theatre from birth.

Born in 1847, she was the daughter of two 'strolling players,' Benjamin and Sarah Terry, and four of her eight surviving siblings also became actors. Ellen could not recall: '[…] when it was first decided that I was to go on the stage, but I expect it was when I was born, for in those days theatrical folk did not imagine that their children could do anything but follow their parents' profession.'

Ellen did not receive a formal education, but she was rigidly drilled in the movement skills and clear elocution required for a career on the stage. Her training could take place at any time and anywhere and she often got up in the middle of the night to rehearse lines and gestures in front of the mirror.

Early roles

Ellen made her first appearance on stage in 1856, aged nine, performing the role of Mamillius in *The Winter's Tale* alongside the actor/manager Charles Kean as Leontes. Her costume included a 'little red-and-silver dress' and 'very pink [and baggy] tights', and she had vivid memories of the pride inspired by her beautiful 'property' – a toy cart. This first performance was nearly Ellen's last, however, as in her eagerness to obey Kean's command to 'go play' she tripped over the handle of her cart, falling flat on her back. Mortified by this disaster, Ellen was certain that her career as actress was ruined forever.

Fortunately, the critics proved willing to overlook the accident and Ellen spent three years as part of Kean's company, performing in Shakespearean productions, melodramas and pantomimes and leaving only when Kean's management of the Princess Theatre ended in 1859.

Then aged 11, Ellen spent the next four years gaining further experience. This included performing with her elder sister, Kate, in a series of touring 'entertainments' and, between 1862–3, working with a stock company in Bristol. Stock companies were troupes of actors connected to a particular theatre, often putting on a different play each night.

By 1864, Ellen had a thorough grounding in Shakespeare, Burlesque and Melodrama and had learned the valuable lesson of 'usefulness'. As she declared: 'Not until we have learned to be useful can we afford to do what we like. The tragedian will always be a limited tragedian if he has not learned how to laugh. The comedian who cannot weep will never touch the highest levels of mirth.'

Left Ellen (right) as Mamillus in *The Winter's Tale* alongside Charles Kean as Leontes

Above right A decorated performance souvenir of *The Winter's Tale* on 28 April 1856

Far left A playbill for *The Winter's Tale* at the Princess's Theatre, London, dating from 1856. This was the performance in which Ellen made her first stage appearance

International celebrity

In 1864 Ellen left the stage to marry the painter, G. F. Watts. The marriage failed within a year however, and she went back to acting. Deeply unhappy and frustrated with her life, in 1868 she abandoned her family and her career to spend six years living with the architect and designer, Edward William Godwin.

Ellen's reluctant return to the stage in 1874 was prompted primarily by financial necessity (the bailiffs were frequent visitors to the homes Ellen shared with Godwin in both London and the countryside). But Ellen remained a consummate professional and the Bancrofts' 1875 production of *The Merchant of Venice,* in which she played Portia for the first time, signalled a crucial shift in her fortunes. As she recalled, 'My fires were only just beginning to burn. Success I had had of a kind, and I had tasted the delight of knowing that audiences liked me, and had liked them back again. But never until I appeared as Portia at the Prince of Wales's had I experienced that awe-struck feeling which comes, I suppose, to no actress more than once in a lifetime—the feeling of the conqueror. In homely parlance, I knew that I had "got them" at the moment when I spoke the speech beginning, "You see me, Lord Bassanio, where I stand."'

By 1878, Ellen Terry was regarded as one of the foremost actresses in London. This success brought her to the attention of Sir Henry Irving and led to an invitation to become the leading lady of the Lyceum Company. Their stage partnership would last for over two decades and led to Ellen becoming an international celebrity,

Hiördis.

'charming' audiences throughout England and beyond. At the peak of her success, she was one of the highest paid actresses in England, and Lyceum Company productions attracted large audiences and received great critical acclaim.

After the Lyceum

By 1902 Ellen, now entering her mid-fifties, had become conscious that the 'Lyceum reign was dying' and with much sadness made the decision to leave the company.

Eager to establish that she was not simply '[…] a "Victorian" actress, lacking in enterprise, an actress belonging to the "old school",' Ellen decided to venture into independent management. She took out a lease for the Imperial Theatre and, in partnership with her son, progressive designer and director Gordon Craig (see p. 18), and her daughter, respected costumier Edy Craig (see p. 14), she staged Ibsen's early work, *The Vikings at Helgeland*. Though liked 'by the artists' and deemed 'beautiful' by Ellen, the bleak setting and gloomy tone of the controversial play did not appeal to the wider public and the production was forced to close.

A revival of one of her most popular roles, Beatrice in *Much Ado About Nothing,* did recoup some of her most serious financial losses, but Ellen regretfully acknowledged that she '[…] singed [her] wings a good deal in the Imperial limelight.' Despite the Imperial's failure, she remained resolute in her belief that the production '[…] anticipated the scenic ideas of the future by a century […].'

Official recognition

Ellen continued to act on stage, and in some early films, until the mid-1920s, at which point ill health, and increasingly poor eyesight, led to her enforced retirement.

The extent of the affection she inspired in the public was evident in the scale of the celebrations that marked her 50 year Stage Jubilee in 1906. It was not until 1925, however, that her status within the theatrical profession received royal recognition and she was finally made a Dame Grand Cross of the British Empire (30 years after Henry Irving had been awarded his knighthood).

This honour provided an official, and longed-for, testament of Ellen's pre-eminent position within her profession and contribution to the arts. When she died in 1928, aged 81, thousands mourned the passing of an actress who had entranced audiences across the world for over 60 years.

Opposite Ellen Terry as Hiördis in *The Vikings at Helgeland*, depicted by Pamela Colman Smith, 1903. The original costume for this role, made by her daughter Edith 'Edy' Craig, survives in the collection at Smallhythe

Left Ellen Terry (right) and Edy Craig. This was a postcard commemorating the day that Ellen was made a dame in 1925

Below The programme for Ellen Terry's 50-year Stage Jubilee in 1906. Calling her 'England's Greatest Actress', the programme reads, 'Women will love her that she is a woman more worthy than any man: men that she is the rarest of all women'

Life off stage

For her first 16 years, Ellen experienced a nomadic existence, constantly moving from one set of theatrical lodgings to another and focusing all her energy on training for a career in the theatre.

Her marriage in 1864, to the painter George Frederick Watts (a man nearly thirty years her senior) propelled her into a 'world full of pictures and music and gentle, artistic people'. While Ellen was fascinated by the illustrious figures she encountered in this new environment – the poet, Alfred, Lord Tennyson among them – there was little room for another woman in Watt's life. As she soon discovered, her husband was closely guarded by his three patrons and protectors, Lady Somers, Sara Prinsep and Juliet Cameron. Popularly known as Beauty, Dash and Talent, the Pattle sisters monopolised both Watts himself and the 'salons' for which their home, Little Holland House, became famous. Insecure, and unprepared for this battle, the teenage Ellen found herself '[…] shrinking and timid, in a corner—the girl-wife of a famous painter […] more of a curiosity, of a side-show, than hostess to these distinguished visitors'.

Perhaps unsurprisingly, the couple separated within a year. In need of an income, Ellen was advised by her parents to return to the stage. She did so reluctantly, and was dissatisfied and depressed by this turn in her fortunes: 'This was the period when, though every one was kind, I hated my life, hated every one and everything in the world more than at any time before or since.'

Edward William Godwin

It was during this bleak period that Ellen renewed her acquaintance with Edward William Godwin whom she had first met in 1862, while working with the Bristol stock company (see p. 6). A leading figure in the burgeoning Aesthetic movement, Godwin impressed and inspired Ellen. She was awed by his house, with its 'sense of design in every detail' and credited the architect and designer with opening her eyes to 'beautiful things in art and literature'. A relationship with Godwin offered not only the romance missing from Ellen's marriage to Watts, but a chance to return to the beautiful surroundings to which she had learnt to aspire.

While Godwin (recently widowed) was free to marry, Ellen, although separated from Watts, was not yet divorced. Her decision to abandon her theatrical career and live, unmarried, with Godwin, was a significant departure from convention and necessitated a potentially irrevocable break with her family and society. Confident in her love for Godwin, Ellen remained undeterred: 'Perhaps it was because I knew they would oppose me that I left the stage quite quietly and secretly … I was troubling myself little about what people were thinking and saying. "They are saying—what are they saying? Let them be saying!"'

A rural idyll

Ellen spent six years living with Godwin in rural Hertfordshire and their relationship had a lasting impact on her taste and views on design. Godwin introduced Ellen to the artistic principles of Aestheticism, a movement strongly influenced by non-European and historical styles. Its followers rejected the conventions governing late 19th-century art, dress and interior design: promoting the idea of 'art for art's sake', celebrating the individual, and stressing the importance of being surrounded by beautiful

things. Godwin drew much of his inspiration from the simplicity and craftsmanship of Japanese art and design. The homes he and Ellen shared were shaped by this minimalist aesthetic – the floors bare or lined with straw matting, the walls plain or decorated with Japanese paper fans and prints – and Ellen herself frequently appeared in a silk kimono.

One of the primary strains on their relationship was the fact that Godwin's work necessitated frequent absences from home and there was often no way for him to warn Ellen that he would be late, or even not returning at all. In 1869, the couple's first child, Edith (Edy) was born. Godwin was absent for this, and the subsequent birth of their son, Edward (Teddy), in 1872.

Edy and Teddy provided Ellen an outlet for her love and energy and she devoted her attention to looking after them and managing the household. It took her some time to adapt to this domestic existence and she learnt by trial and error – the aroma resulting from cooking a chicken without removing its 'innards' providing a lasting memory.

Opposite Ellen Terry aged 17, as painted by her then-husband G. F. Watts. She is wearing the brown silk wedding dress designed for her by William Holman Hunt. Entitled *Choosing*, it shows her torn between the showy (but scent-less) camellias and the delicate but more sweet-smelling violets clutched in her left hand. It was a symbolic reflection of the choice Ellen made when she gave up the notoriety of the stage for a quiet life with Watts in the same year this was painted (National Portrait Gallery website)

Above Ellen with her children, Edy and Teddy, c. 1886

Love and letters

Although Ellen '[…] was very happy, leading a quiet, domestic life in the heart of the country […]' with Edward William Godwin, practical concerns, not least, the large discrepancy between the couple's expenditure and income, began to intrude upon this idyllic existence.

By 1874 it was apparent that another source of funds was required, and Ellen agreed to return to London and to life as an actress. Within a year, their already fragile relationship had begun to collapse and Ellen soon found herself the family's sole source of income.

The 'fallen woman'

Ellen had returned to London and society as a 'fallen woman'. Her elder sister, Kate, had retired from the stage and, respectably married, refused to receive her. Even Ellen's parents were reluctant to accept their disgraced daughter. This pressure to re-establish a position in society may have been one factor in Ellen's decision to make a second marriage, this time to a fellow actor, Charles Clavering Wardell, who acted under the name Charles Kelly. Ellen met Wardell during the original run of *Olivia* at the Court Theatre in 1877. Watts finally filed for divorce that same year and Ellen married Wardell soon after.

The marriage enabled Ellen to re-establish contact with her family, and her children were given temporary 'legitimacy', becoming Edith and Edward Wardell. Ellen soon discovered, however, that not only did Wardell drink to excess, but he was also jealous, and potentially violent. Ellen's increasingly close relationship

MR. CHARLES KELLY.

A SOUND ACTOR.

with her new on-stage partner, Henry Irving, put her marriage under even greater strain. Soon the actress asked Wardell to leave, offering him three-quarters of her weekly earnings in return. They eventually separated completely in 1881. Even though the Married Women's Property Act was passed the same year Ellen continued to support Wardell, and his family, until his death from alcoholism four years later.

Above left 'A Sound Actor', a character of Charles Wardell, or Kelly, by Alfred Bryant, taken from 'Enteracte', date unknown

Above right Ellen Terry and James Carew at Smallhythe Place, in what is now the Terry Room

Opposite A letter sent from Ellen to James Carew

Twenty-nine years Ellen's junior, Carew was a controversial choice for the actress's third, and final, husband. But handsome, kind, and somewhat in awe of his celebrated wife, Carew offered Ellen security and admiration at a time when she feared losing both.

For a time, both appear to have been happy. Practical concerns soon took their toll however; Carew found it increasingly difficult to find work, while Ellen, as the primary earner, was keen to retain her independence. Further emotional pressure was exacted on the relationship by the estrangement it created between Ellen and her daughter. Close to and protective of Ellen, Edy resented the marriage (not least because it had taken place in secret, when Ellen was on tour in America). She locked the gate between the two cottages and the lock remained in place whenever Carew was in residence, until Carew and Ellen agreed to an amicable separation in 1909.

Although they no longer lived together, Carew's and Ellen's friendship endured. 'Jim' remained part of Ellen's life, helping to care for the actress in her final years. He was among the mourners at her funeral in 1928 and Ellen left her 'good-man' a legacy of £200.

James Carew

Although there were certainly rumours about their affair, Irving and Ellen took great care to conceal the true nature of their relationship (see pp. 30–33). Not long after Irving's death in 1905 however, Ellen's personal life once again attracted scandal when, in March 1907, she married the American actor James Carew.

Edith Craig (1869–1947)

Edy Craig was the first child born to Ellen Terry and William Godwin.

Both parents were keen to instil 'appropriate' Aesthetic taste and values in their children from a young age (Edy's brother, Edward was born in 1872). As Ellen explained in her autobiography, 'They were allowed no rubbishy picture-books, but from the first Japanese prints and fans lined their nursery walls, and Walter Crane was their classic … Only wooden toys were allowed. This severe training proved so effective that when a doll dressed in a violent pink silk dress was given to Edy, she said it was "vulgar"!'

Ellen, whose career necessitated late nights and frequent travel, was keen to provide stability for her children and give them access to the 'real education' she had been denied. She sent them, from a young age, to a school run by Mrs. Cole, a supporter of the new women's movement, who '[…] believed that girls should be as well educated as boys'. Ellen also later encouraged her daughter to apply for university, but when Edy failed to pass the necessary examination, sent her to study music in Germany. Edy was a promising pianist, studying the piano both here and at the Royal Academy of Music in London, but sadly her career was halted by the rheumatism she began to experience in her hands.

What's in a name?

The question of what surname her children should take remained a dilemma for Ellen for much of their childhood. In the end it was a trip to Scotland and the famous rock, Ailsa Craig, which provided the required inspiration: shortly afterwards both her children adopted the surname Craig.

Edy on stage

Having lost the chance of a musical career, Edy looked to the theatre. In 1890 she returned from studying music in Berlin to join the Lyceum Company. She initially performed minor roles, and often stood in for her mother (whom she resembled) in scenes such as the prologue to the 1895 production of *King Arthur*, where Ellen, who freely confessed that 'Fidgeting was one of [her] worst faults', was required to remain still for long periods.

Edy spent nearly ten years working at the Lyceum, taking part in their tours to America and establishing herself as a useful member of the company. During the last seven of these years Edy also worked independently with other prominent actors, amongst them George Alexander and Stella (Mrs Patrick) Campbell. Her mother's connections also helped Edy find work, and in 1897 Bernard Shaw, with whom Ellen was then in regular correspondence, arranged for Edy to take part in tour productions of his own play, *Candida* and Ibsen's *A Doll's House*.

Opposite Ellen and Edy as a child, c. 1883

Above Ellen and Edy in Henry Irving's production of *Henry VIII* at the Lyceum, 1892

Edy behind the scenes

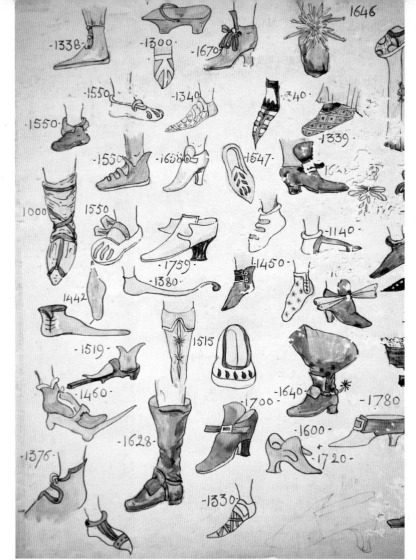

Edy's work as an actress played an important part in her subsequent career as a costumier, as it put her in direct contact with many of the performers for whom she subsequently made and designed costumes.

Her skill as a costumier first became apparent during her time at the Lyceum. For the role of Jessica in *The Merchant of Venice,* for instance, her costume consisted of an ingenious arrangement of 'scarves and bits and pieces' held together with safety pins. She also had a lifelong habit of collecting images and sketches in scrapbooks, which provided a valuable reference guide for her professional work.

The turning point in Edy's career was the 1899 Lyceum production of *Robespierre.* Henry Irving, who had gradually become aware of Edy's flair for costume design, commissioned her to re-design the costumes and they were judged to be a great success.

With financial support from her mother, Edy sought to capitalise on this success by starting a business as a theatrical costumier in Covent Garden. In 1900 she designed and supervised the making of all the costumes for Laurence Irving's interpretation of *Bonnie Dundee* at the Adelphi Theatre and the following year she created the costumes for Lillie Langtry's productions of *Mademoiselle Mars* and *The Sacrament of Judas.* Sarah Bernhardt was also among Edy's clients and she continued to design and make costumes for her mother, both during her time at the Lyceum Theatre and in the years which followed.

'My daughter has acted also—not enough to please me, for I have a very firm belief in her talents—and has shown again and again that she can design and make clothes for the stage that are both lovely and effective. In all my most successful stage dresses lately she has had a hand, and if I had anything to do with a national theatre, I should, without prejudice, put her in charge of the wardrobe at once!'

Ellen Terry on Edy Craig in her autobiography *The Story of My Life,* 1908

Edy the director

Until recently, Edy's pioneering role as a stage director had often been overlooked. Between 1911 and 1921, her talent as a director enabled her to play a leading role in the productions staged by the campaigning theatre group that she was instrumental in establishing, the Pioneer Players (see p. 49). Her career as a director pre-dates this however, and she was achieving recognition as early as 1907. She produced several of Bernard Shaw's plays at Hampstead's Everyman Theatre in the 1920s, spent two years as Art Director at the Leeds Art Club and worked for the Renaissance Theatre Society. Her work was respected by performers, dramatists and critics, who praised its 'pictorial quality' and 'visual impact'.

Shaping her mother's legacy

While Edy's status within theatre history has seldom received the recognition it merits, she took great care to ensure her mother wouldn't be forgotten. From 1928 onwards, she dedicated much of her time and energy to securing the future of Smallhythe Place and sustaining her mother's legacy (see p. 23).

Edy's final days

In March 1947, Edy defied the advice of her doctors and braved freezing weather to attend the service at St Paul's Church, Covent Garden (known as The Actors' Church) to commemorate her mother's birth. Already frail and suffering from a heart condition, Edy nevertheless refused to stop work. A few days later, and in the midst of planning the annual Shakespearean production for the Barn Theatre (see p. 53), she had a sudden, and fatal, heart attack.

Opposite A selection of shoes from various dates, as sketched by Edy Craig

Top right Edy Craig in bed with a cat (said to be 'George'), painted by her partner Clare 'Tony' Atwood in 1943, oil on canvas

Above Edy in a Bath chair at Smallhythe (Bath chairs were light, one-person, hand-pushed carriages with folding hoods; they were named after their place of origin, Bath in Somerset, but could also be said to look similar to an old-fashioned bathtub)

Edward Gordon Craig (1872–1966)

Ellen Terry's son, Edward Henry Gordon Craig, was a precocious child whom, as Ellen noted, everyone adored because he was 'fat, fair and angelic looking'.

First known as simply Edward, he became known as Edward Gordon after he was baptised in 1883. Though domineered by his confident older sister, who exhorted her more nervous sibling to 'be a woman', the young 'Master Teddy' was certainly capable of charming his admirers and retained this talent throughout his life.

Despite his evident intelligence, Gordon Craig's school career was not a great success and his formal education ended in 1888 when 'misconduct' resulted in his expulsion, a punishment his mother thought too severe.

A career on the stage (1885–97)

The end of Gordon Craig's education marked the commencement of his stage career. In 1889 he joined the Lyceum Company, the company with whom he had made his stage debut, in their 1885 American Tour. He performed alongside his mother twice and in 1896 took on the role of Hamlet, wearing Irving's original costume.

Designing and directing

Although Gordon Craig's acting was well received, his primary interest lay in forging an independent career as a designer and director and he left the Lyceum Company in 1897 to pursue this aim.

In 1900, he designed a production of *Dido and Aenaeas* for the Purcell Society. His work was revolutionary for stage and set design, breaking with the tradition of stage realism and using light and colour to evoke mood and movement. Two years later he was invited to work on a production of Handel's *Acis and Galatea* and in 1903 he collaborated with his mother and sister to design and direct Ibsen's *The Vikings*.

While artists and performers recognised his talent, Gordon Craig's modernist approach failed to win over English theatregoers and Gordon Craig turned to Europe for a more appreciative audience. Accepting the invitation of diplomat, writer and art enthusiast Count Harry Kessler to visit Germany, he moved to Berlin in 1904 and rarely returned to England thereafter.

Around this time Gordon Craig began to publish articles and books setting out his theories on stage design. The best known of these was *The Art of the Theatre* (1905). In 1908 he founded and edited his international review, *The Mask,* which remained in print until 1929 and helped to make his theatrical ideals widely known.

He later moved from Germany to Italy, settling in Florence where he established a School for the Art of Theatre. While living in Italy, he invented the portable folding screens used in set designs for his famous co-production of *Hamlet* with Stanislavsky, which was presented at the Moscow Art Theatre in 1912 to great critical acclaim.

Later career

The advent of the First World War resulted in the closure of Gordon Craig's school in Italy and a hiatus in his stage career. Although he continued to design and direct productions after 1918, his demand for complete artistic control restricted his opportunities for employment (not least because he gained a reputation for being difficult to work with).

Undaunted, Gordon Craig turned his attention to theatrical history and became increasingly interested in documenting not only his own ideas and work, but also that of his predecessors – among them, Sir Henry Irving, about whom he published a biography in 1930.

In 1931 Gordon Craig moved to France; he was interned there during the Second World War and continued to live there after the War ended. In 1957 he published his memoirs, *Index to the Story of My Days,* and the following year was awarded an OBE for his contribution to the theatre. During his final years, Gordon Craig lived in increasingly straitened circumstances and he died in 1966, aged 94.

Legacy

Although many of the productions Gordon Craig designed were never staged – and the few that were seldom achieved popular success – he had a significant and enduring impact on attitudes to stage design in early 20th-century theatre. His lectures, published writings, and the etchings and woodblock prints with which he documented his research and ideas secured his legacy and have ensured that Gordon Craig remains a highly regarded figure in the field of stage design.

Opposite Gordon Craig playing Alexander Oldworthy with his mother playing the title character in *Nance Oldfield,* which opened in 1891 at the Lyceum

Above Gordon Craig's costume designs for 'The Torchbearers, and 'Egil' in *The Vikings at Helgeland*

Teddy and his family

As Gordon Craig spent much of his adult life abroad, he rarely visited Smallhythe Place. Ellen kept in close touch via letter however, and her son made occasional trips down to Kent when in England, often with his family.

Photographs capture one visit he made with his first wife and the mother of four of his children, actress Helen Mary (Mae) Gibson, whom he married in 1893. Later images document a return to Smallhythe, this time with his second long-term partner, Elena Meo, and two of their children. Despite appearing relaxed and happy in these pictures, Gordon Craig appeared to struggle to leave his work entirely; in a photograph from 1910, he is positioned in front of one of his stage designs.

A mother's support

Even though his writings and stage productions achieved greater recognition and respect in Europe, Gordon Craig still struggled to make a living, and continued to rely on financial support from his mother. His life was complicated further by the gradual collapse of his first marriage and the series of affairs which followed. He divorced Helen Gibson in 1905, having begun an affair with the violinist Elena Meo (1879–1957) two years earlier. His relationship with Meo continued until her death in 1957, and they had three children together. Even so, he had at least two further serious affairs, the first, in 1905, with the dancer Isadora Duncan and another in the 1930s, with Daphne Woodward. He also had several more

children, including daughters by both Duncan and Woodward.

While she might have disapproved of the way her son conducted his personal relationships (particularly the lack of concern he showed for his ex-partners and children), Ellen remained fiercely proud of his professional achievements. She also provided practical help, often having her grandchildren to stay at Smallhythe Place and not only gave Gordon Craig a generous allowance, but also helped to fund the care of many of his children.

Opposite Gordon Craig with his then-wife Helen Mary (Mae) Gibson and three children around a bonfire at Smallhythe, August 1902

Above left Gordon Craig working on one of his set models at Smallhythe in 1910

Above right Elena Meo in front of the sitting room windows in Smallhythe's garden, 1923

Left Gordon Craig, his second long-term partner Elena Meo and two of their children Ellen (Nelly) Craig and Edward (Little Teddy) Craig sit on the steps of Smallhythe with a dog, date unknown

Ellen Terry and Smallhythe Place (1899–1928)

'My own house, bought with my own money'

Ellen Terry's professional life was inextricably connected with the cities and provincial towns in which she performed. The countryside offered her a refuge from the pace and pressure of her work and, as her celebrity grew, a rare opportunity for privacy.

Although Ellen's principal home was always in London, she rented and owned a number of 'country cottages' over the course of her life. Among her more unusual residences were a pub near Uxbridge – at which the terms of her lease required her to act as a publican (fortunately she had very few customers) – and her 'first wee cottage' at Hampton Court where her children re-enacted scenes from Shakespeare in the palace grounds. She spent the longest period living at Tower Cottage in Winchelsea, East Sussex and at Smallhythe Place (then called the farm – it was only called Smallhythe Place after Ellen's death, although it's thought it had also been called this name in the past, before Ellen's time). Both houses provided her with a vital retreat from London and the stage.

It was while exploring the marshlands between Rye and Tenterden with Sir Henry Irving that Ellen Terry first discovered Smallhythe Place.

When asked if it 'was a nice house', the shepherd living there bluntly responded, 'No'. Undaunted, Ellen immediately decided that this was where she would like to live and die. When the house and surrounding land were subsequently sold at auction, she purchased both. She also rented and later bought the house next to the church for Edy, and then bought Yew Tree Cottage opposite Smallhythe Place in 1914.

A refuge in the countryside

Smallhythe was a convenient place for Ellen to live. Trains from nearby stations reached London in just two hours. It was an easy journey for visitors and during the summer Ellen, who did not like travelling by train, could leave the theatre at midnight and drive her pony and trap through the night to arrive at daybreak.

When she first bought Smallhythe Place, it was in a poor state of repair. Over the decades, it was transformed into a comfortable home. Ellen was proud of the home she had created, not least because she had worked independently to earn the money required to purchase it. For her it was, and remained, a testament to her success: '[...] my own house, bought with my own money'.

A memorial

Ellen left all her remaining property at Smallhythe to Edy. Despite limited funds, Edy remained determined to establish Smallhythe Place in honour of her mother. Following a failed national appeal to raise £15,000 to preserve the house as a memorial, Edy used her own financial resources, bolstered by generous donations, to turn the house into a museum and transform the neglected barn into a theatre. The house opened to the public in mid-1929, and the Theatre was opened as a private membership club.

Financial pressures prompted Edy to approach the National Trust for additional support in 1938. The following year the Trust agreed to take on

'Smallhythe Place, the unpretentious old timbered farm house about which there still seems to hang some of the old shimmering iridescence that was Ellen Terry [...]'

Edith Craig and Christopher St. John, *Ellen Terry's Memoirs*, 1932

the property, subject to Edy retaining a life interest. Edy remained at the neighbouring Priest House until her death in 1947. The house was formally handed over to the Trust in 1949 by Edy's life partners, Christopher St John and Clare ('Tony') Atwood (see pp. 48–51).

A constant presence

Edy rearranged many of Smallhythe's rooms to create displays relating to Ellen Terry's life. Similarly, although some of the actress's personal effects were sold after her death, the vast majority of the items remaining in the house originally belonged to Ellen. With the exception of the Library, which was created in 1968 (see p. 34), and the recently re-designed Costume Room (see p. 40), the current layout of the rooms departs very little from Edy's original arrangements. Smallhythe Place therefore survives much as E. V. Lucas described in 1936: filled with mementoes of Ellen Terry's life and career, and still 'pulsating with [her] personality'.

Opposite A view of the house at Smallhythe

Above Ellen Terry and a friend, thought to be Violet Pym, in a coster cart at Smallhythe Place, taken some time between 1900 and 1928. Coster carts were the type typically used by fruit and vegetable sellers

The Terry Room

Used by Ellen as a sitting room, the Terry Room now explores the actress's connections with the leading artists and performers of her generation and documents key moments in her 60-year career.

Much of the furniture is original to the room. A 1907 image, for instance, shows Ellen and her third husband, James Carew, seated at the round table that stands in the centre of the room. Also of interest is the small mahogany tea table. Sometimes referred to as 'The Smallhythe table', it was designed for Ellen by Godwin in c. 1872 and exemplifies his elegant and restrained approach to interior design.

Family and friends

The room contains numerous images of Ellen, several of them paintings connected with her first husband, G. F. Watts. Ellen was a dedicated model and sat for so long wearing the heavy armour depicted in *The Watchman, What of the Night?* (c. 1867) that she fainted.

The costume sketches

Above the fireplace are sketches by Watt's contemporary and fellow Pre-Raphaelite, Edward Burne-Jones. Burne-Jones, a friend of both Ellen and Irving, designed the set and costumes for the 1895 Lyceum production of *King Arthur* and these images show his initial ideas for two of the costumes Ellen was to wear as Guinevere.

Ellen and Oscar

Among the interesting theatrical items in the cabinets is a letter from an aspiring playwright: Oscar Wilde. Written in 1880, when Wilde was in his mid-20s, he sent it to Ellen accompanied by a copy of his first play, *Vera,* and expressed his hope to one day, 'write something worthy of [her] playing'. Although Ellen never appeared in any of Wilde's plays, their admiration and friendship was mutual, and the actress described him as 'one of the most remarkable men' she had ever known.

Personal memorabilia

The room also contains more intimate mementoes of Ellen's life. These include a record of her birth registering her full name, Alice Ellen Terry, and a copy of her family tree. Another interesting object is the 'friendship necklace', now divided into five separate strands, which Ellen compiled from the beads given to her by fellow performers, close friends and family members. Among the contributors were her costume maker, Ada Nettleship (see p. 42), the American actress Pauline Chase, and Ellen's elder sister Kate, grandmother to Sir John Gielgud.

Professional mementoes

The room also contains reminders of Ellen's professional achievements. A scroll produced to commemorate her 50-year Stage Jubilee in 1906 runs across the top of the fireplace. The celebrations staged to mark this event attracted huge crowds, who queued through the night to obtain tickets for the benefit performance at the Theatre Royal Drury Lane. Leading figures in the arts from across England, Europe and America gathered to pay their respects to Ellen. The then Undersecretary of State for the Colonies, Winston Churchill presided over the Jubilee banquet and paid tribute to an actress who had 'elevated and sustained the quality and distinction of theatrical art in England'.

Also on display is the gold insignia with which Ellen was presented when she was made a Dame Grand Cross of the British Empire. This title – the highest level of award for merit by the Crown – was not established until 1917, and Ellen was only the second actress to receive the honour. Ellen was by this time nearly blind, and increasingly fragile. Nevertheless, she insisted on curtseying before the monarch and prepared a short speech for the occasion, observing: 'I am delighted. It is an honour to my profession, an honour to women, and very pleasant for me.'

Above left *'Watchman, What of the Night?'*, a portrait of Ellen Terry in armour and clutching a sword c. 1867 by her first husband, G. F. Watts and now on display at Smallhythe

Above right Just some of Ellen's collection of friendship beads, each given to her by a friend. They were originally made into a necklace, but now sit in five separate strands. The seven beads here are from (top to bottom) Vera Catchpole, Ella Overbeck, 'Bo', Bobbie Hamilton, Emily Shaw, Pauline Chase and Ada Nettleship

Left Ellen Terry's Golden Jubilee celebrations at the Drury Theatre, 12 June 1906

Above centre A view of the Terry Room

The Dining Room

Still retaining elements of the private social space this room once provided for Ellen, the Dining Room now offers an insight into the theatrical world within which she rose to prominence.

Originally the kitchen, this room was turned into a Dining Room by Ellen when she arrived at Smallhythe Place. It was a sociable, informal space: somewhere to gather companionably together around the fire as the weather grew colder. Ellen's wooden settle has retained its position to the right of the 16th-century fireplace.

Ellen, influenced by the homes she shared with both Watts and Godwin (see pp. 10–11), steered clear of the chintz that dominated many Victorian homes. Smallhythe's rooms retained their polished wooden or brick floors, enlivened by the occasional patterned rug. Although some concessions to tradition were made, in general Ellen, holding fast to Aestheticism's veneration of the unique, individual and beautiful, furnished her houses to suit her own tastes and needs, rather than to conform to current fashions.

A public memorial

Today this room reflects Smallhythe Place's new identity and its conversion from a private home to a public memorial: the cases, with their handwritten labels, were originally installed by Edy Craig.

Ellen was an avid collector of theatrical memorabilia connected with both her own career and that of her colleagues and predecessors.

Ellen and Whistler

Displayed on the large, open-shelved dresser against the back wall is Ellen's collection of willow-pattern china, thought to have been given to her by James McNeill Whistler. Ellen was introduced to the painter by Godwin when the Aesthetic movement and its celebration of 'art for art's sake', was just becoming established in London. Both this 'blue and white china' and the silk kimono Whistler presented to their daughter, Edy (possibly pictured right), were key accessories for members of the Aesthetic movement, particularly, those, who, like Godwin and Whistler, drew inspiration from the simplicity and craftsmanship that characterised Japanese art and design.

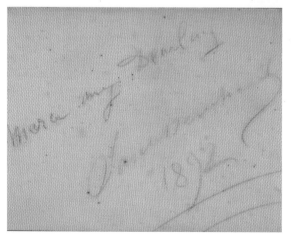

Playbills lined the staircase in her home in Chelsea and when living in Earl's Court, her 'case of curios' included a bible used by the famous 18th-century actress Sarah Siddons. It was her daughter, however, who brought all these objects together. Both the freestanding cabinets and the walls in this room are filled with pieces drawn from this extremely diverse collection. The joint creation of mother and daughter, the collection on display here, and throughout the house, documents Ellen's respect for the actors who inspired her as a child, and the continuing deference she felt towards her fellow performers even after she had earned her own position within the 'theatrical aristocracy'.

The role models
Among the actors featured on the walls are the actor/manager Charles Kean, in a print of him as Hamlet, alongside whom Ellen made her first stage appearance. A neighbouring image shows his wife, née Ellen Tree, as Rosalind in *As You Like It*. Both had a significant influence on Ellen's stage career, the latter providing a formidable, but instructive, role model for the eight-year-old actress.

On another wall is a note from Ellen's friend and contemporary, the famous French performer, Sarah Bernhardt: 'Merci my Dearling' scrawled in greasepaint across her dressing table cloth, left to thank Ellen for the loan of her dressing room.

The glass cabinets
The curiosities contained within the glass cabinets include an inkstand owned by another actress Ellen greatly admired, Eleanora Duse, and an eyeglass used by Sir Arthur Sullivan, who composed incidental music for several Lyceum productions. While the majority of these cases focus on the individuals who inspired Ellen, the mementoes they contain reaffirm the status she achieved within her profession and recall the actors and artists who became both colleagues and friends.

Trinkets from travels
Ellen's fame was not confined to England: the actress visited America on seven tours with the Lyceum Company between 1883 and 1902. The small display case containing souvenirs from these tours gestures towards her status as an international celebrity.

Above The Dining Room at Smallhythe Place, as depicted by Tony Atwood c. 1920, oil painting on canvas

Left The willow-patterned china, thought to have been gifted to Ellen by Whistler

Far left Sarah Bernhardt's thank-you note to Ellen

The Lyceum Room

Previously used as a bedroom, this room now offers an insight into Ellen's stage career, particularly from her time at the Lyceum theatre.

The glass-fronted cabinet standing against the far wall contains a particularly varied range of mementoes from Ellen's many performances, including a pair of satin slippers she wore as Titania in *A Midsummer Night's Dream* in 1863. Godwin designed Ellen's dress for the production and he showed her '[…] how to damp it and "wring" it while it was wet, tying up the material […] so that when it was dry and untied, it was all crinkled and clinging'. For Ellen, the costume stood out as '[…] the first lovely dress that I ever wore' that she 'learned a great deal from'.

Also on display are props, sketches and photographs connected with Sir Henry Irving, including photographs of his beloved terrier, Fussie, who had a special chair in his dressing room at the Lyceum and was a faithful, if indulged, companion to his master.

'Early Days at the Lyceum'
Irving became manager of the Lyceum Theatre in 1878 and, in need of a leading lady, invited Ellen to join the company. Keen to make the Lyceum both respected and profitable, Irving knew that in Ellen he had a talented actress whom audiences were keen to see perform.

Ellen first performed with the Lyceum Company in the 1878 production of *Hamlet*: Irving played the title role and Ellen was Ophelia. Even at this early stage in their partnership, Irving allowed Ellen a significant degree of control over the designs of her costumes. This confidence in his new leading lady nearly proved disastrous however, as Ellen, keen to reflect her character's deteriorating state of mind, selected a transparent black material for Ophelia's final scene. Fortunately, Irving's production advisor, Walter Lacy was on hand to inform the actress that 'there must be only one black figure in this play, and that's Hamlet!' Ellen was horrified by her mistake, and quickly commissioned a replacement costume. The incident had a lasting impact on her approach to costume design at the Lyceum: although she '[…] knew more of art and archaeology in dress than [Irving] did, he [often] had a finer sense of what was right for the scene'.

'A Temple of Art'

Although Ellen had been convinced of its failure, the 1878 production of *Hamlet* proved to be the first in a series of triumphant successes for the company. It was swiftly followed by more Shakespearean productions and Irving's historical dramas also proved popular, as did the 1885 adaptation of *Faust*. The success of these performances, coupled with the vast sums Irving invested in the sets and costumes, soon established the Lyceum's reputation as a 'Temple of Art' and 'A Theatre of Beauty'.

'The Twilight of the Gods'

Among the company's most famous productions was the 1888 staging of *Macbeth* and, although Ellen's performance as Lady Macbeth proved controversial, she felt it to be one of her greatest roles. It was to prove one of her last triumphs with the company however, and in her autobiography Ellen dates the gradual decline of the Lyceum Company to around this point.

Above A view of the Lyceum Room

Left Props from *Macbeth*

Right Ellen Terry's white satin ballet shoes, which may have been a part of her costume for Titania in *A Midsummer Night's Dream*, a part she played aged 16. Ellen considered dance integral to the craft of an actor and in 1913 she would publish one of the first books on the Ballets Russes, an influential Russian ballet company

When Ellen was 45, she was persuaded to play Cordelia in *King Lear*, even though it was a role her sister Kate had performed aged 14. Sustaining the illusion of 'eternal youth' became an increasingly oppressive burden for the actress. There were still fleeting moments of brilliance: Ellen's performance as Imogen in *Cymbeline* in 1896 was 'accounted one of her greatest triumphs'; although aged 50, Ellen was described as 'full of girlish spirits'. Yet, Ellen believed this production represented her 'only inspired performance of these later years'. Two years later almost the entire stock of scenery held by the company was destroyed in a fire, and Irving's financial problems worsened as returns from performances declined. By 1902, Ellen was conscious that the theatre (now being run by a syndicate) was under serious financial strain.

Conscious that, however forgiving her audiences were, she could no longer provide the youthful and innocent heroines Irving required, Ellen made the reluctant decision to leave the Lyceum Company. Her final stage appearance with Irving was in July 1902, playing Portia to his Shylock in *The Merchant of Venice*.

Sir Henry Irving (1838–1905)

Born as John Henry Brodribb, Henry Irving came from a working-class background and was the son of a travelling salesman. He was initially trained for a career as a clerk, but, despite family opposition, his true vocation remained the stage.

Irving never had any formal training. He built up his experience by performing in amateur productions and took lessons in fencing and acting. With very limited funds to spare, he used a £100 legacy from his uncle to invest in tights, swords, wigs, boots and period coats and hats: essential equipment for an aspiring actor at the time. Unusually tall and very thin, Irving also swam regularly in the Thames to build up his physique (he was particularly self-conscious about his legs and, until Ellen advised him not to, used to bulk them out with padding).

These investments paid off. Aged 18, Irving obtained his first formal theatrical engagement in Sunderland. He appeared under the name he had adopted by Royal licence in 1889: Henry Irving. This was a change he made in deference to his mother, who, as a fervent Methodist, objected strongly to her son's choice of profession.

Irving spent the next ten years in the provinces working with various stock companies and a further five working at theatres in London, acquiring the experience needed to earn a long-term engagement with the Batemans' Company at the Lyceum Theatre in 1871. Irving then served another seven years' apprenticeship with the Batemans and, finally, began to achieve widespread success. Audiences' first insight into

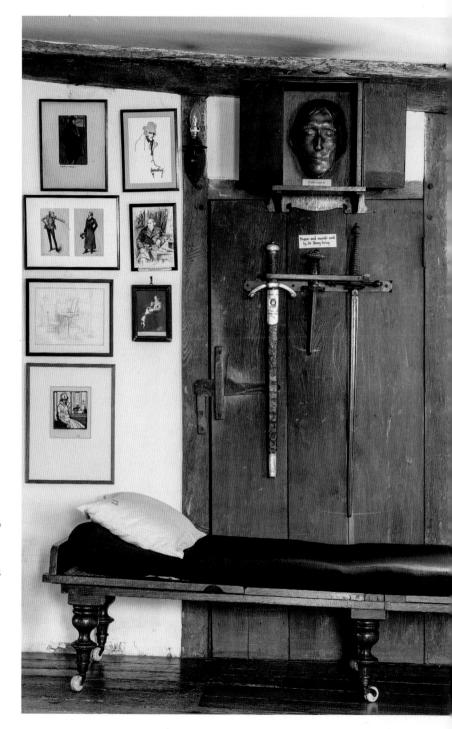

Irving's talent was his haunting rendition of the guilt-stricken Mathias in *The Bells* (1871). It was his compelling characterisation of Hamlet in 1874, however, that secured his position at the forefront of his profession; a role which, as Ellen declared, proved to be 'by far the greatest part that he ever played, or was ever to play'. Four years later Irving was confirmed as one of the leading actors of the day and he had risen to a position where he could take over the management of the Lyceum.

The Lyceum Company

Although their stage partnership officially commenced in 1878, this was not the first time Ellen and Irving performed together. However, their first joint stage appearance – in David Garrick's 'reduced version' of *The Taming of the Shrew* in 1867 – was not a great success. Neither enjoyed the performance: Irving described Ellen as 'charming and individual as a woman, but as an actress hoydenish!'. Ellen appreciated Irving's commitment to the profession but felt his performance lacked 'technical skill' and that they had both 'played badly'. In the decade since, however, both had revised their opinions, and Ellen's acceptance of Irving's invitation to become the leading lady of the Lyceum Company in 1878 marked the beginning of a professional partnership that was founded on mutual respect and endured for over 20 years.

Ellen gave Irving practical help, persuading the actor, who was always nervous before going on stage, to '[…] give up that dreadful, paralyzing waiting at the side for his cue'. As she explained, '[…] after a time he took my advice. He was never obstinate in such matters. His one object was to find out, to test suggestion, and follow it if it stood his test'.

There were occasional differences of opinion, but a compromise was generally reached and, as Ellen observed, 'for one thing I did not like doing at the Lyceum, there would probably be a hundred things I should dislike doing in another theatre'.

Irving's achievements
Among Irving's greatest achievements were the international tours he mounted between 1883 and 1904. Irving transported his entire London productions across North America and Canada, including actors, sets, costumes and musicians – something never previously attempted.

SOUVENIR of MACBETH
PRODUCED AT THE
LYCEUM THEATRE
BY HENRY IRVING
Decr 29th 1888.
Illustrated by CHA^s CATTERMOLE, R.I. AND J. BERNARD PARTRIDGE.
Price ONE SHILLING.

Above Henry Irving by Ernest Walter Histed, 1899

Opposite Henry Irving mementoes, including his death mask, in the Lyceum Room

Left The cover from a souvenir of *Macbeth*, a production Henry Irving staged at the Lyceum in 1888

Irving off stage

Another of Irving's great achievements was behind the scenes. He mounted a sustained campaign to establish acting as a respectable profession and to secure theatre as an 'art form' worthy of recognition among the great 'arts'. He lectured widely on the subject, becoming the first actor to lecture at the Royal Academy Banquet and at Oxford University.

His knighthood, awarded in 1895, was testimony both to the importance of his stage career, and also the progress he had made towards achieving his ambition.

Irving's relationships

Irving married Florence O'Callaghan in 1869. They had two children together, Laurence and H. B. Irving, both of whom went on to have careers on the stage. Sadly for Irving, his wife was deeply ashamed of his profession; after witnessing his triumphant performance in *The Bells,* she reportedly asked 'Are you going on making a fool of yourself like this every night?' Unsurprisingly the pair separated, but Florence, a Catholic, refused to divorce Irving.

Consequently Irving could never marry Ellen Terry and their love affair (documented in surviving letters) had to remain secret. Although Irving was a frequent visitor to Ellen's homes, they were conscious that discovery would provoke public condemnation and could destroy their careers. They therefore took great care to maintain a professional distance when appearing together in public, even staying in separate hotels on their American tours.

Over time however, their relationship broke down under this strain, and by 1900 Irving had begun an affair with the journalist, Eliza Aria. Aria became Irving's companion during the final years of his life and, together with his two sons, was one of the few beneficiaries of his will.

Above *Whay a Knight We're Having*: David Garrick congratulating Sir Henry Irving on his knighthood, by Edward Linley Sambourne, dated 1 June 1895. On the reverse is a copy of the cartoon from Punch, inscribed by Ellen Terry 'Given to E.T. by H.I. February 1896'

Final years

Although Ellen and Irving's professional partnership ended in 1902, their friendship endured. Irving continued to work at his usual frantic rate, struggling to recoup the Lyceum Company's lost funds. In 1904 he began a series of Farewell Tours with plans to retire in 1906, after celebrating fifty years on the stage.

His health was beginning to fail, however, and just two hours after appearing as the title role in *Becket* at the Theatre Royal Bradford, Irving collapsed in the foyer of the Midland Hotel. He died on 13 October 1905, aged just 67. His sudden death shocked the nation. It prompted a successful campaign for his burial in Westminster Abbey, and over 40,000 people came to witness the procession of his coffin. His ashes were buried in the south transept, next to the grave of the 18th-century Shakespearian actor David Garrick and in front of Shakespeare's memorial statue.

From the wreath I sent

FUNERAL OF

SIR HENRY IRVING, LL.D., D.LITT.

CHOIR.

Admit *Mrs Ellen Terry*

TO

WESTMINSTER ABBEY,

On FRIDAY, the 20th OCTOBER, 1905,

12 noon.

ALL SHOULD BE SEATED BY 11.30.

J. ARMITAGE ROBINSON, Dean.

Ellen was among the prominent figures who attended Irving's funeral and was devastated by his death. She kept the ticket she received for the ceremony, preserving it alongside a piece of the rosemary from the wreath she sent to the funeral and annotating it: 'All who loved him knew him and all who knew him loved him'.

Left A wreathed rosemary, with a note from Ellen Terry saying it was 'from the wreath I sent' to Henry Irving's funeral, along with her ticket

Above Henry Irving and 'Fussie' the dog in Winchelsea, sometime between 1890 and 1905

The Library

When Ellen was living at Smallhythe, her books were distributed throughout the house, 'mainly just in piles'. It was not until 1968 that this room was converted into a small library within which all the books could be brought together; today more than 3,000 can be found here.

As F. T. Bowyer said in 1977, 'The charm and interest of the books is due largely to their owner's copious comments and annotations'. Ellen's marginalia is present throughout the books here. They include theatrical biographies

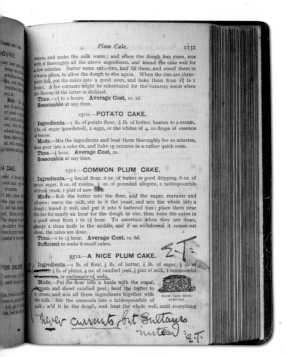

of both her predecessors and contemporaries; play texts (both productions she appeared in, and others she studied); copies of her son's publications on stage design and production; books documenting the history of dress marked up with notes about design ideas, and notes for Ellen's own articles and books, including her series of lectures on Shakespeare.

The vast majority were collected by Ellen. Some titles, primarily theatrical biographies, were added to the collection after her death, among them *Edy: Recollections of Edith Craig,* a collection of essays about Ellen's daughter.

'And one man in his time plays many parts (and so does a woman).'

The motto Ellen Terry composed for her Jubilee performance in 1906

Above A view of Smallhythe's Library

Left *Mrs Beeton's Book of Household Management,* with Ellen's notes in the margins

Opposite Notes Ellen made on her lecture about Shakespeare's heroines

Commitment to her craft

The library is a testament to the painstaking research Ellen carried out when preparing for her stage roles. The annotations that fill the acting copies of her play texts capture her ideas for how she would interpret her roles: thoughts about pace, gesture and tone of voice. They also reveal that the actress, while willing to respect and conform to her directors' decisions, often had her own strong opinions about the most effective way to present certain scenes.

Among the most interesting, and heavily annotated, items in the collection are the manuscripts of the lectures Ellen presented on Shakespeare across Britain, America and Australia between 1910 and 1914. Written in collaboration with her ghostwriter and 'literary henchman' Christopher St John (see p. 48), the typeface has been intentionally enlarged to make it big enough for Ellen, whose eyesight was already beginning to fade, to read without spectacles. Despite this, the text is barely legible, as it is covered in Ellen's handwritten stage directions, crossings out and additions. As St John recalled: 'When [Ellen Terry] first delivered the lecture … she adhered more or less faithfully to the original version. By 1915 she had transformed it with cuts, transpositions, and the incorporation of many of her platform improvisations'. Ellen

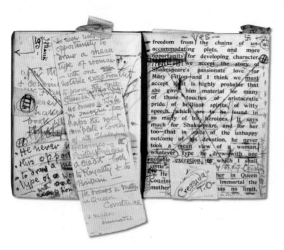

From *Four Lectures on Shakespeare*, 1932

'I have played Beatrice hundreds of times, but not once as I know she ought to be played. I was never swift enough […] But at least I did not make the mistake of being arch and skittish, and this encourages me to think I could have played Rosalind well.

'I have been Beatrice! Would that I could say "I have been Rosalind". Would that the opportunity to play this part had come my way when I was in my prime! I reckon it one of the greatest disappointments of my life that it did not! In my old age I go on studying Rosalind, rather wistfully I admit.'

also worked with her daughter to create a suitable scene and costume for her 'performances': appearing alongside a lectern (previously used as a desk by Irving) and wearing 'flowing robes of crimson, or white or grey,' – the colour chosen to suit the lecture's mood.

Of the four lectures, it was those on Shakespeare's heroines that proved most popular. These provided the actress with a chance to revive some of her most famous performances, and to take on some of the roles she had never had the opportunity to perform.

The legacy of Ellen Terry

This library has a crucial part to play in not only sustaining but challenging Ellen Terry's legacy. It is filled with a sense of the actress's presence and voice. The knowledge, experience and passion behind the marginalia filling Ellen's books still resonates today and within their pages you come into direct contact with the vibrant personality that 'charmed' audiences for over 50 years. Most significantly, these texts provide definitive proof that, as Ellen stated, 'There [was] something more in my acting than charm!'.

The Bedroom

The Bedroom is perhaps the most intimate and personal space in Smallhythe Place, and its layout reflects the way Ellen used the room.

The atmosphere of tranquillity and calm owes much to the complete absence of objects connected with Ellen's professional life and celebrity status. The focus is instead on the actress's off-stage life as a daughter, sister, mother and a woman in her own right.

The furnishings

The furniture here was not chosen to impress, but because it had a personal connection to Ellen, or served a practical purpose. The round table, still laid for tea, reflects how, in later years, this room became both her sitting room and bedroom. Positioned next to the window, with its view of the hedge, road and Yew Tree Cottage beyond, is the dressing table Godwin (see p. 11) once designed for her. The well-worn original school desk next to this dressing table was used by Ellen throughout her life, having originally been purchased for her children.

The paintings and photographs

The paintings and photographs lining the walls are of Ellen's family and the people to whom she felt closest. Among them is a pastel portrait of her mother, Sarah Terry. While Ellen confessed to being her father's 'particular pet', and remained close to him throughout her life, she also had great affection and respect for her mother. As she wrote in her autobiography, 'I can well imagine that the children of some strolling players used to have a hard time of it, but my mother was not one to shirk her duties. She worked hard at her profession and yet found it possible not to drag up her children, to live or die as it happened, but to bring them up to be healthy, happy, and wise—theatre-wise, at any rate'.

The pastel portrait of her mother sits between two similar portraits of Ellen's own children, and further images of both Edy and Teddy are present throughout the room. As both these pastel portraits, and the large head and shoulders mounted in round frames on the opposite wall, reveal, Ellen ensured her children were dressed in the height of Aesthetic fashions.

Above Ellen's dressing table in her bedroom, still set out with her belongings

Opposite, above A view of Ellen's bedroom

Opposite, below Ellen sat at the old school desk that she would use throughout her life; this photograph was taken at her home in Barkstone Gardens, London

The Bedroom: 'Puzzledom'

During her final months at Smallhythe, Ellen's bedroom was moved downstairs, into the space now known as the Terry Room (see p. 24).

Ellen's final years

Although she still gave occasional performances into the 1920s, Ellen was beginning to retire from the stage. She made her final appearance in Walter de la Mare's *Crossings* in late 1925. Much to her frustration, the only stage directions Ellen received were to 'come on' and then 'go off'. Even so, Christopher St John declared that the awestruck 'Oh' with which the audience greeted the great actress's arrival on the stage was '[…] a more wonderful tribute than any applause'.

Ellen's final years were a period of gradual decline. The award of her damehood in 1925 was certainly a highlight, even though the actress was so overcome by the excitement of the ceremony that she '[…] quite forgot to walk out backwards!'. The Royal laughter which greeted this realisation, recaptured, for an instant, the merriness that had characterised Ellen's youth, but the stark reality was that her increasing 'forgetfulness' was becoming a cause of concern not only to the actress herself, but also to all those who cared for her.

Imprisoned in a state Ellen referred to as 'Puzzledom' she was, perhaps fortunately, scarcely aware that the vast sums she had earned during her celebrated career were now dwindling away to a point where she was on the verge of bankruptcy.

Although there were flashes of her old charm, humour and generosity, Ellen was often irritable and increasingly difficult to live with. It became almost impossible to retain servants, until Edy Craig discovered Hilda Barnes, who cared for Ellen until her death.

'I am unhinged (not unhappy) and uncomfortable, I wondered where everything is. Cannot remember new things. All is changed. Change at 73 puzzles the will. I live in puzzledom.'

Ellen Terry, writing in her diary, April 1921

No funeral gloom

'I hate being old. Yes, I just hate it. People are very kind, but that makes it worse. However, it's absurd to cry over spilt milk. I intend to go into my grave smiling,' determined Ellen Terry in 1928. During her final months, except for a few short excursions in her wheelchair, Ellen spent much of her time inside, though the windows were left open to let in the scents and breeze from the garden during what was a very hot July. On the morning of 17 July, Ellen had a sudden stroke. Barnes fetched St John and Atwood from the nearby Priest House and a telegram was sent to Edy, who had gone up to London the day before. By pure chance, Gordon Craig was also in London and both children rushed back to Smallhythe Place.

Ellen never fully recovered consciousness. She eventually died peacefully on the morning of 21 July, her family at her bedside. Ellen's death sparked a wave of national mourning, and the Royal Family were among those who sent telegrams to Edy expressing their deep sadness at the loss of such a great actress. In accordance with Ellen's wishes that there should be 'no funeral gloom', everything was kept very simple and the guests were asked to dress in their brightest clothes. Covered in a 'golden pall' that Edy had created from the remains of an old stage costume, the coffin – designed by Gordon Craig – was carried in front of the colourful procession, which Ellen's children led up the road to the nearby church. At the church entrance the mourners passed through a guard of honour, formed by local farmworkers and their sheepdogs. A year later, in July 1929, the actress's ashes were installed in St. Paul's Church, Covent Garden, known as The Actors' Church, in London, where they remain today.

No Funeral Gloom

'No funeral gloom, my dears, when I am gone,
Corpse-gazing, tears, black raiment, graveyard grimness.
Think of me as withdrawn into the dimness,
Yours still, you mine,
Remember all the best of our past moments and forget the rest,
And so to where I wait come gently on.'

A poem by William Allingham, written out by hand by Ellen Terry

Above Ellen Terry's funeral procession walking past Priest House, 1928. Edward Gordon, Edy Craig and James Carew can all be seen

Opposite above Gold insignia for the Dame Grand Cross of the British Empire, awarded to Ellen Terry in 1925. Conceived in 1917, the title was the highest level of award for merit by the Crown and Ellen was the second actress to receive the honour

Opposite below Ellen Terry and her nurse and companion Hilda Barnes at Smallhythe during the final years of Ellen's life. Hilda was affectionately known to the family as 'Barney'

The Costume Collection

Ellen paid close attention to all the elements of her stage performances, but she attached specific importance to the design and creation of her costumes.

Over one hundred of these costumes have survived as part of the collection at Smallhythe Place and can be seen in the Costume Room. They date primarily from her time at the Lyceum Theatre (1878–1902), although some are later, including costumes from the 1903 productions of *The Merry Wives of Windsor* and *A Winter's Tale*, both made by Edy Craig.

The collection also includes costumes worn by other performers, among them a greatcoat used by her brother, Fred Terry, when playing Sir Percy Blakeney in *The Scarlet Pimpernel* in 1905. Ellen also kept some of Henry Irving's costumes, including the brown silk – velvet doublet and matching trunk hose created for his performance as Benedick to Ellen's Beatrice in *Much Ado About Nothing* (1880) and a set of the silk crimson robes he wore for the role of Cardinal Wolsey in *Henry VIII* (1892) – the silk was sent to the Cardinal's College in Rome to be dyed exactly the right shade of red.

Sir Henry Irving as Cardinal Wolsey.

'Beautiful and fat to-night'

Unusually tall for a woman of this period (about 5ft 10in), Ellen was extremely self-conscious about her height and large hands, particularly as a teenager. Over time however, she learnt to overcome these insecurities, and while never achieving the 'daintiness' she admired in others, became renowned for her graceful, gliding movement, both on and off the stage.

When she first joined the Lyceum Company, Ellen was extremely thin and her dresser, Sally, would reassure the actress with the 'terse compliment', 'Beautiful and fat to-night, dear'. By her final years with the company, an improved diet and income meant that Ellen's figure was significantly fuller. A change was therefore made in the compliment, and Sally would assure Ellen that she looked 'Beautiful and thin tonight' instead.

The oldest

The oldest costume in the collection is a dress Ellen wore as Ophelia in *Hamlet* in 1878. This costume, though not particularly beautiful, marked her first appearance as the leading lady of the Lyceum Company. As she recalled in her autobiography, 'My Ophelia dress was made of material which could not have cost more than 2s. a yard, and not many yards were wanted, as I was at the time thin to vanishing point! I have the dress still, and, looking at it the other day, I wondered what leading lady now would consent to wear it'.

Opposite Henry Irving as Cardinal Wolsey in Henry VIII in 1892, and a pin cushion Ellen made using the red material from his robes

Right Ellen Terry as Ophelia in *Hamlet*

1878. OPHELIA.

'There is something, I suppose, in a woman's nature which always makes her remember how she was dressed at any specially eventful moment of her life, and I can see myself, as though it were yesterday, in the little red-and-silver dress I wore as Mamillius.'

Ellen Terry, 1908

Creators and collaborators

The level of control Ellen was able to exercise over her costumes while the leading lady of the Lyceum Company was unusual.

Part of Irving's willingness to trust Ellen's 'judgement about colours, clothes and lighting' may have stemmed from her past training, as the actress observed 'I had learned from Mr. Watts, from Mr. Godwin, and from other artists, until a sense of decorative effect had become second nature to me'.

The time Ellen spent with Watts and Godwin had a clear impact on her approach to design both on and off the stage. She openly acknowledged the enduring influence of Watt's teaching on her understanding of art and credited Godwin with initiating her 'interest in colour, texture, effects of light on colour, the meaning of dress, and a certain taste for beauty which [she] never lost'.

Conscious of the importance not only of creating beautiful costumes, but of ensuring that they suited the backdrop against which they would appear she worked closely with the scene painters, consulting them about the colour of her costumes '[…] so that I should not look wrong in their scenes, nor their scenes wrong with my dresses'.

Alice Comyns Carr

From the mid-1880s, Ellen collaborated closely on her costumes with Alice Comyns Carr. Though Comyns Carr was already working for the company from about 1882, the first production over which she had full control was the 1887 adaptation of *The Amber Heart*. The soft pleats used to shape Ellen's flowing robes were reputedly achieved in a rather an unorthodox manner: twisting the fabric of the dress 'up into a ball and boil[ing] it in a potato steamer'.

Comyns Carr also introduced Ellen to Ada Nettleship, who would go on to design many of her most successful costumes. Dressmaking offered Nettleship a means by which to supplement the slender income brought in by her husband's painting. By 1900, thanks to her partnership with Ellen, and demonstrable talent as a costumier, she had earned a reputation as one of the 'most unique' dressmakers of the period.

Above *Mrs. J. W. Comyns Carr* painted by John Singer Sargent in c. 1889, now on display in the Speed Art Museum, Kentucky

Opposite, left Ellen as Katherine of Aragon in *Henry VIII*, 1892

Opposite, right Ellen as Ellaline in *The Amber Heart*, 1887. This was the first production over which Comyns Carr had full control of the costumes

The art of wearing dresses

As Ellen soon learnt, the success of a costume depended in part on the performer's ability to move gracefully while wearing it, and she spent many hours practising the 'uprightness of carriage and certainty of step' required to manage her 'trailing skirts'. Being able to move gracefully and appropriately in her costumes remained a priority for Ellen; Alice Comyns Carr regretfully observed, that though possessing 'a fine sense' of historical dress,' the actress would 'jib at fashions that she fancied might interfere with her movement while acting'.

'Ellen Terry is an enigma. Her eyes are pale, her nose rather long, her mouth nothing particular. Complexion a delicate brick dust, hair rather like tow. Yet somehow she is beautiful. Her expression kills any pretty face you see beside her. Her figure is lean and bony, her hands masculine in size and form. Yet she is a pattern of fawnlike grace, whether in movement or repose.'

Charles Reade of Ellen Terry, c. 1887

After the Lyceum

On her departure from the Lyceum Company in 1902, Ellen looked to a new designer for her costumes, collaborating with her daughter Edy Craig. Edy had already contributed costumes to Ellen's stage wardrobe during her final years at the Lyceum and now had a costume workshop at Covent Garden.

Edy's 'real genius'

The 1902 production of *The Merry Wives of Windsor* at His Majesty's Theatre, in which Ellen appeared as Mistress Page, presented Edy with an opportunity to display both her creativity and resourcefulness. She began by rescuing Ellen from the 'black panne velvet dress' in which she was asked to perform, creating a 'red and yellow' costume far better suited to the 'rollicking, farcical comedy'.

Midway into the run of the production there was a fire in Ellen's dressing room and the following morning it was discovered that her costume was burnt 'to a cinder'. Undaunted, Edy called in 'all hands' and had a replacement costume at the theatre by 7pm that same night.

Ellen declared that 'Edy has real genius for dresses for the stage' explaining that, 'My dress for Mrs. Page was such a real thing – it helped me enormously – and I was never more grateful for my daughter's gift'. In 1960, Sybil Thorndike described how 'Ellen's stage clothes became such a part of her that some magic seemed to belong to them. I know her daughter Edith Craig never liked them being cleaned, she said it spoilt them and the magic went out of them'.

> 'My daughter says to know what not to do is the secret of making stage dresses. It is not a question of time or of money, but of omission.'

Ellen Terry, 1908

After retirement

As Ellen's stage appearances decreased, she and Edy were very willing to lend her costumes to fellow performers and friends. In 1910, for instance, Ellen lent the crimson silk robes she had worn as Portia to Vita Sackville-West to wear at a Shakespeare Masque staged at Knole, Kent (now also National Trust) and in 1921 Sybil Thorndike borrowed the 'beetlewing dress' for a performance as Lady Macbeth. After Ellen's death the costumes were worn in several Barn Theatre productions and to publicise fundraising events.

Opposite Tony Atwood's portrait of Vita Sackville-West in Ellen Terry's 1895 costume for Portia in *The Merchant of Venice,* which was staged at Knole in July 1910

Right Ellen in Edy Craig's striking costume for Mistress Page in *The Merry Wives of Windsor,* 1902

Above Wreaths made for a pageant devised by Edy Craig c. 1930

MISS ELLEN TERRY.
AS "MISTRESS PAGE"

5540 B

ROTARY PHOTO

Collection highlights

Although no longer worn, these costumes still retain an element of the 'magic' that Sybil Thorndike attributed to them. They are now carefully preserved in the stable loft that was once Tony Atwood's studio, but there are also always some on display in the Costume Room.

The beetlewing dress

Among the costumes Ellen ranked as 'Mrs. Nettle's greatest triumphs' was the famous 'beetlewing dress' that she and Alice Comyns Carr created for Ellen to wear as Lady Macbeth in 1888. The costume was a highlight of the original production and it remains famous today, having been immortalised in an 1889 John Singer Sargent painting.

The annotations filling both reference books and the copy of Ellen's script for the production record the painstaking research that inspired the costume. The silhouette referenced 11th-century engravings and the dress was cut to a pattern which Comyns Carr found in 'the wonderful costume book' by Eugène Viollet-le-Duc. Comyns Carr's aim was to create a dress as 'like soft chain armour as I could, and yet have something that would give the appearance of the scales of a serpent'. The costume was therefore constructed from panels of a fine yarn Nettleship had purchased in Bohemia, which had 'a twist of soft green silk and blue tinsel' running through it.

However, despite the eerie glow offered by the crocheted soft green silk and blue tinsel bodice, the dress was still not felt to be 'brilliant enough'. The solution came from iridescent 'beetlewings', the wing covers of European and Asian jewel beetles (Buprestidae), which they shed naturally and were used on dresses and accessories in the 19th century, particularly for fashionable evening wear. They also proved ideally suited to the 'thick softness of gaslight with the lovely speaks and motes in it'. With the further addition of 'a narrow border in Celtic designs, worked out in rubies and diamonds' at the hem and sleeve cuffs, the costume was finally complete.

'The street that on a wet and dreary morning has vouchsafed the vision of Lady Macbeth in full regalia magnificently seated in a four-wheeler can never again be as other streets: it must always be full of wonderful possibilities.'

Oscar Wilde, describing Ellen Terry arriving at John Singer Sargent's studio to be painted in the beetlewing dress

'One of the loveliest dresses'

Irving frequently employed leading artists within the Aesthetic movement to design some of his most spectacular productions. The Dutch painter Sir Lawrence Alma-Tadema was responsible for another costume Ellen remembered with special fondness: a dress designed for her performance as Imogen in the 1896 production of *Cymbeline*.

The costume, which survives in the collection at Smallhythe, had a softly pleated bodice of pale cream and sea-green silk gauze. This was paired with an asymmetrical skirt, draped in folds from Ellen's right hip and constructed from panels of purple, orange, russet and gold twill silk. The success of the costume, both as a work of art and a garment specifically tailored to suit the taste and figure of the actress, is apparent in surviving images. Ellen described it as '[…] one of the loveliest dresses that I ever wore'.

Opposite, right and left Ellen as Lady Macbeth in the beetlewing dress, and a close-up detail from that dress

Above A Liberty-style tea dress, possibly dating from the 1870s. While not a stage costume, this remains in the collection and is possibly an early example of the artistic/Aesthetic movement of dress reform. This style favoured loose, un-corseted, free-flowing dresses based on the ideals of ancient Greek fashions, with which Ellen was associated with in London

Right Ellen as Imogen in *Cymbeline*, 1896

Independent Women

Alongside Ellen Terry, Smallhythe Place is testament to the lives of three equally important women: Edy Craig, and Edy's two partners, the novelist and dramatist Christopher St John and the painter, Tony Atwood.

'Edy and her boys' lived at the neighbouring Priest House for over six decades. All three women played a crucial part in the story of Smallhythe Place, and in preserving not only the house, but also Ellen Terry's legacy.

Christopher St John

Christopher Marie St John was born Christabel Gertrude Marshall. For some years, she acted as secretary to Lady Randolph Churchill and, occasionally, to her son Winston Churchill.

St John (who greatly admired Ellen's performances) first encountered Edy by chance in 1895, when visiting Ellen Terry in her dressing room at the Lyceum, but they didn't meet properly until early 1899. Ellen, who had maintained a correspondence with St John, invited her to supper and asked Edy to help entertain their visitor. Anticipating an enthusiastic fan and potential nuisance, Edy's welcome was far from warm, but St John, who found herself strongly attracted to Edy, was undaunted by

this reception and the feeling soon became mutual. By autumn that year, Edy and St John had decided to look for a house together. Their relationship lasted until Edy's death in 1947.

The writer

St John also established a professional relationship with Ellen, working as her ghostwriter on many articles and her memoirs, *The Story of My Life* (1908). They also collaborated on Ellen's 'Four Lectures on Shakespeare'. Not revealing her involvement until after Ellen's death, St John consistently stressed Ellen's leading role in the creative process.

St John was a respected playwright and novelist in her own right, too. Her first novel, *The Crimson Weed,* was published in 1900. The semi-autobiographical *Hungerheart: The Story of a Soul,* begun in 1899 and published anonymously in 1915, is one of her most personal works, drawing inspiration from St John's involvement in the Suffrage Movement and also providing insights into her relationship with Edy Craig. St John also took the lead in publishing *Ellen Terry and Bernard Shaw: A Correspondence* in 1931, which helped raise funds for the Ellen Terry memorial. Responding in part to Edward Gordon Craig's biography of his mother, *Ellen Terry and her Secret Self* (1931), St John and Edy also worked together on a revised and extended edition of Ellen Terry's memoirs (1932).

Suffrage and the Pioneer Players

Edy and St John also had similar political sympathies and both became involved in the Suffrage Movement. St John wrote plays and articles in its support and, though not always a militant suffragette, in 1909 she was arrested for setting fire to a pillar box.

St John also became part of the Women's Social and Political Union and was a committee

member of the Catholic Women's Suffrage Society and the Women Writers' Suffrage League. She and Edy both acted in the first production of *A Pageant of Great Women* in 1909. Devised by Edy with the actress and writer Cicely Hamilton, the play celebrated women's achievements across the centuries and was performed nationwide.

Edy was a member of the Women's Freedom League and the Actresses' Franchise League. She also established the Pioneer Players in 1911 and directed many of the 63 productions staged by the company.

The Pioneer Players was known for its support of progressive political and social movements. This included the campaign for women's suffrage, but their remit extended beyond this to encompass 'all kinds of movement of interest'. They promoted foreign playwrights, translating plays by figures such as Paul Claudel, Anton Chekhov and Herman Heijermans, and provided an important platform for female dramatists from the past and present, Hamilton and St John among them. Although the company soon established a reputation for innovative and relevant productions, it struggled to become financially stable. By 1921 it was apparent the cost of producing performances could no longer be covered by membership subscriptions and the company was officially disbanded.

Opposite above Christopher St John (second left), Cicely Hamilton (centre) and Edy Craig (right) marching in support of the Women Writers' Suffrage League

Opposite below Edy Craig with Christopher St John and Tony Atwood

Right The production of Edy's play, *A Pageant of Great Women,* in 1909

The Smallhythe triptych

Tony Atwood (1866–1962)

It was while working for the Pioneer Players that Edy Craig met Clare Atwood. A professional artist, Atwood, later known as Tony, trained at Slade School of Fine Art and, from 1893, exhibited her work at the New English Art Club, becoming a member in 1912. She produced some of her most significant paintings in response to the First World War, during which she was commissioned by the Women's Work Sub-Committee of the Imperial War Museum to produce pictures depicting the work of the Women's Voluntary Service (WVS). She also worked in the theatre and joined the British Drama League's committee in 1919.

Both Atwood and St John were involved in the Pioneer Players, St John as a dramatist, translator and actor and Atwood as a set designer and prop maker. Edy and Atwood took increasing pleasure in each other's company and, in 1916, Edy invited Atwood to join her and St John in Smallhythe. Although keen for Atwood to join them, Edy was very conscious of St John's often passionate emotions and insecurity – St John's suicide attempt in 1903 was prompted by Edy's short-lived engagement to the musician, Martin Shaw. Edy therefore warned Atwood: '[…] if Chris does not like your being here, and feels you are interfering with our friendship, out you go!'.

Fortunately for all three, Atwood's arrival strengthened, rather than threatened, Edy's relationship with St John. Atwood became a peacemaker, dispelling any potential tension and bringing much-needed calm and stability to their London homes and the Priest House.

Above Tony Atwood's self-portrait, 1951

Opposite, right *The Terrace outside the Priest House* by Tony Atwood, 1919. The painting depicts (from left to right) Christopher St John; Olive Morris, (Mrs Charles Chaplin);

Anthony Hawtrey; Edy Craig and Ellen Terry. Edy's little black cat, Snuffles, looks on

Opposite, left Edy Craig and Chris St John c. 1910–16, photographed with Edy's camera

A ménage à trois

The success of this unusual ménage à trois stemmed in part from the fact that all three women remained active within their own – interconnected – spheres of expertise. Though committed to, and often distracted by, their professional careers, the women enjoyed teasing one another and their homes were noisy and busy environments – the peace frequently interrupted by heated, but affectionate, debates about domestic problems, politics and books.

The trio formed a nexus of support and social activity for actors, women and the lesbian community in Kent and Sussex throughout the 1930s and 1940s. They were particularly supportive of Radclyffe Hall and her partner Una Troubridge (who lived in nearby Rye) following the obscenity trial of Hall's novel *The Well of Loneliness*.

Descriptions of life at the Priest House and the private scenes captured in surviving photographs, suggest that this was a fun, creative and intimate space: a place in which all three women, and all those connected with them, felt secure and loved.

'[…] This is a triptych, not a single portrait. On either side of Edy hang the panels representing Tony and Christopher […] The talents distributed between the three are varied and manifold […] Christopher is […] the inspiring genius of the garden and perhaps, although she does not know it, the most romantic character of the three […] Tony floats between them. Perhaps she has not always had an easy time. She is small, she is brave, she has a gift for drollery, she is a peacemaker, she restores the balance […] This does not mean that Tony is a soft buffer, […] bouncing unselfishly between the more violent personalities of Edy and Christopher. No Tony is a person on her own. This is the remarkable thing about them; all three of them are still persons on their own. Strong personalities living at such close quarters for so many years, yet none of them has been extinguished by the other […]'
– Vita Sackville West, 'Triptych' in *Edy: Recollections of Edith Craig*, ed. Eleanor Adlard, 1949

The Barn Theatre

In 1929, Edy Craig turned Smallhythe's small barn into a theatre that is still used today.

Ellen, for whom Smallhythe Place provided an important escape from London and the stage, repeatedly rebuffed suggestions that she should create a theatre there. The 17th-century barn in the grounds of the house, although used occasionally for storage, remained somewhat neglected and overlooked. After Ellen's death however, Edy seized her opportunity and began to transform the building into a working theatre and a memorial to her mother.

'[…] it is a strange mixture of the professional and amateur, of gaiety and sadness – the ease of a country garden party and the solemnity of a tribute to a great artist […] it is amazingly fitting and right. I believe Nell would have loved it as much as you do. It expresses much of her character through you, in the same way as her cottage still does, and her lovely garden, and her spirit which surely moves about the place wherever one goes.'

John Gielgud, writing to Edy Craig in the 1930s.

The performances

Finances were stretched, but with assistance, Edy created a stage at the west end. Seating, originally comprised of rough benches on a beaten earth floor, was positioned in front. The cast and crew had to make creative use of the resources available: red fire buckets were placed beside the stage, performers 'dressed in the cottage', and the production's lighting consisted of detached car headlights placed in biscuit tins.

The first performance took place on 21 July 1929, the first anniversary of Ellen Terry's death. It was the first in a series of annual memorial performances. These 'memorial matinees' would be rehearsed in London (under Edy Craig's direction) before opening at Smallhythe for a single performance. In recognition of Ellen Terry's status as a 'Shakespearean actress', the matinees would generally include scenes from Shakespeare. There would also be an address paying tribute to the actress and, after her death, to Edy Craig.

On several occasions performers wore Ellen's original costumes, including the ninth memorial matinee in 1937, which featured an appearance by Violet Vanbrugh as Katherine of Aragon. Vanbrugh wore the costume Ellen had worn for the 1892 production of *Henry VIII*: a heavy, black silk-damask robe trimmed with fur.

The Barn Theatre Society

Improvements were continually made to the theatre and the original benches were soon replaced with 100 rush seated chairs. Edy sold the chairs to patrons for £1, the 15-shilling profit making an important financial contribution to the theatre. A lighting rig was also created, from which posies of sweet peas were often hung.

From 1929–47, Edy took primary responsibility for the productions staged here, presenting at least five plays each summer. Acting as director, she collaborated with Christopher St John, who focussed on the writing, and Tony Atwood, who painted and constructed the scenery. Edy's network of theatrical contacts enabled her to entice star performers down to Smallhythe. St John and Atwood also performed in several productions. They also assisted with the 'sumptuous buffet' provided afterwards (generally beer, cider, lemonade and sandwiches).

In 1931, the Barn Theatre Society was formed. Members paid a subscription fee, and were entitled to attend all performances except the annual memorial performance, which remained by invitation only. The quality and originality of Edy's productions established the Barn Theatre as a dramatic centre, a status it retained until the outbreak of war in 1939 enforced a temporary halt to performances.

Opposite, above Smallhythe's barn theatre

Opposite, below Dating from 1939, this oil painting shows Edy in the Barn Theatre with her solicitor Irene Cooper Willis (seated) and Charles Staite (on ladder). Staite was an actor who lived in Smallhythe during the War; he was the only person Edy allowed to live there after Ellen Terry died

Above left Christopher St John, Olive Terry and Tony Atwood in their costumes ready for a performance, from scrapbooks compiled by Edy Craig

Above right Another image from Edy's scrapbooks, showing Violet Vanbrugh as Katherine of Aragon, wearing Ellen Terry's original costume from the 1892 Lyceum production of *Henry VIII*

The Smallhythe performances

Since 1919, hundreds of shows have been staged at Smallhythe. These included 33 performances directed by Edy Craig, 15 presented by the Ellen Terry Fellowship and 102 produced by Anthony Thomas, director from 1961 until the 1990s.

The Ellen Terry Fellowship

Following Edy's death in 1947, the Ellen Terry Fellowship was formed. Working under the chairmanship of Sir Lewis Casson and with Sir John Gielgud as President, the Fellowship's sole purpose was to ensure the continuation of the annual matinee performance (see p. 53). The National Trust granted the Fellowship lease of the barn on a small rent and, until 1960, they continued to present the annual memorial matinees. St John and Atwood, who had continued to live at the Priest House after Edy's death, managed the seating allocation and 'general well-being of the guests'. St John also prepared a 'magnificent floral trophy' which was arranged in the 'great silver loving cup'.

'The Ellen Terry Theatre Club'

In 1961 the Ellen Terry Fellowship was dissolved and Antony Thomas was appointed to manage the theatre. Under his leadership the Ellen Terry Theatre Club took over the responsibility of 'continuing the tradition of live theatre at the Barn'. Although it proved impossible to maintain the custom of the grand memorial matinees with their cast of famous London performers, most of the shows staged at Smallhythe were still produced by professional companies.

Special performances

The production staged in 1956 – the centenary of Ellen Terry's first appearance on stage – featured 19 short sketches, each depicting one of the actress's greatest roles. The evening was put together by the actress and director Margaret Webster and a number of contemporary stars took to the stage. Star performers included John Gielgud, Dame Peggy Ashcroft, Dame Sybil Thorndike and Irene Worth.

1957 was another special year. Marking the tenth anniversary of Edy Craig's death, the performance consisted of excerpts from ten plays that she had produced between 1900 and 1932.

SOME OF THE PROFESSIONAL ARTISTS
WHO HAVE APPEARED AT THE BARN THEATRE
1948 TO 1969

Nicholas Amer
David Aylmer
Felix Aylmer +
Peggy Ashcroft
Hywel Bennett
Pamela Brown
Martin Browne
Gladys Boot
June Bailey
Jeremy Burnham
Angela Baddeley
Oliver Burt
Lewis Casson +
Iné Cameron
Audrey Cameron +
Jeanne de Casalis +
Joseph O'Conner
Rosalie Crutchley
Clemence Dane
Michael Denison +
Alan Dobie
Carl Dolmetsch
Fabia Drake +
Ruth Draper
Jean Duncan
Robert Eddison +
David Enders
Edith Evans +
Jessie Evans +
John van Eyssen +
Gwen Frangcon-Davies +
David Fithian
Amabel Gibson
John Gielgud +
Dorothy Gordon +

Marius Goring
Alec Guinness
Rachel Gurney
Dulcie Gray +
Richard Hampton
Nicholas Hannen
Paul Hansard
Paul Hardwick +
Elton Hayes
Charles Hickman
Michael Hordern
Basil Hoskins
Gordon Honey
Donald Houston
George Howe
John Humphry
Anthony Ireland
Pauline Jameson
Ursula Jeans
Isobel Jeans
Barbara Jefford +
Margaret Johnston
Margaret Leighton
Lalage Lewis
Roger Livesey
Diana Maddox
David March
David Markham
Ernest Milton
Micheál Mac Liammóir +
James Maxwell
Yvonne Mitchell
Douglas Moodie
Michael Nightingale
Robert Pears

Joan Plowright
Molly Rankin
Honale Raeburn
Margaret Rawlings +
Aubrey Richards
Michael Redgrave
Paul Rogers
Michael Ragnan
George Rose +
Peter Russel
Shaun O'Riorden
Merula Salaman
Peter Sallis
Athene Seyler
Paul Scofield
Margaret Scott +
Norman Shelley
Jean Sterling Mackinlay +
Judith Stott
Reginald Tate
Ernest Thesiger
Sybil Thorndike +
Veronica Turleigh
Irene Vanbrugh
Marda Vanne
Margaret Vines
Margaret Webster +
Simon Ward
Leckwood West
Harcourt Williams +
Peter Williams
Emlyn Williams +
Cecil Winter
Mary Wimbush
Irene Worth

ARTISTS MARKED + HAVE APPEARED HERE MORE THAN ONCE

Above The inside of the Barn Theatre

Above right A list of some of the figures who trod the boards at the Barn Theatre

Improving the building

Just as importantly for the theatre's future, Thomas started making improvements to the building. At this point the theatre had no foyer and audience members entered directly from the field (in those days mown only by sheep). There were no bathroom facilities for either audience or players and no kitchen for refreshments. Consent was obtained to build on a large covered foyer, together with lavatories, a small kitchen and a space for the artists. An apron stage was added to the original stage, some six feet in front of the original curtain line. The central steps, previously positioned at the front of the stage and said to have been 'rescued' from Irving's stock of scenery at the Lyceum Theatre, remained in situ, concealed beneath this projection.

Outdoor performances

Thomas also produced outdoor performances at Smallhythe – a tradition that, weather permitting, still continues. The first outdoor performance, a production of *A Midsummer Night's Dream,* took place in 1970. An area of the garden was raised to create a stage, with the exits and entrances masked by hazel bushes, while The Barn was used for refreshments and a bar.

Performance, events and exhibitions

In 1992, Tony Weare revived the Barn Theatre Society, which has staged four or five productions each year since. In 1997 – 150 years after Ellen Terry's birth – a 'Theatrical Angels Appeal' was launched to raise funds for the theatre. Twenty-two Guardian angels each donated £1,000, among them Sir Paul McCartney and his first wife Linda, and the theatre producer and owner, Sir Cameron Macintosh. Each had their name put on the back of an original rush-seated chair.

When Tony Weare retired in 2003, Peter Mould, whose links with Smallhythe go back to the days of Anthony Thomas, took over as the director of the Barn Theatre Society. He has maintained the tradition of the subscription theatre club, staging five or six plays each year as well as producing the Annual Memorial Performance that still takes place each July to commemorate the anniversary of the death of Ellen Terry.

The Trust's management

In 2004 the National Trust took over the management of the theatre. Improvements have been made to the space, partially digging out the floor to create tiered seating, rebuilding the stage and insulating the Green Room and Dressing Room. We have also introduced a season-long programme of productions by visiting artistes to supplement those of the Barn Theatre Society. Just as Edy Craig envisioned, the Barn Theatre remains an important venue for theatre productions. Its role has also expanded, however, and the building has become a key venue for exhibitions, study days and talks about the collection.

The Garden

'I suppose the yellow jasmine
is all over the place now –
I wish I could be there to see it'

Ellen Terry, writing to her gardener,
Ladd, in 1919

The current layout of the garden aims to recapture the spirit of Smallhythe Place as it was during Ellen's time here. Surviving elements of her original garden – the Rose Garden in particular – have been retained. An emphasis is also placed on making sure the grounds include a diverse range of plants and shrubs and to ensure that the property is haven for both wildlife and visitors.

However, it has proven difficult to trace the precise outline of the garden as it was laid out when Ellen lived here – in part because it may well have been dug up and turned over entirely to vegetables during the Second World War. It's likely that it was not particularly formal in design, and photographs indicate that pergolas (possibly constructed from the hop poles used in neighbouring hop gardens) and poplar trees featured prominently throughout.

One important survival is the Rose Garden, which is known to have been created by Ellen. All the rose varieties still growing within it date from before 1928, including 'The Terry Rose', a yellow rose that was named after the actress when she was made a Dame in 1925.

Letters to Ladd

A cache of letters sent from Ellen to her gardener/handyman, Ladd, between 1919 and 1920 do offer some insights into the management and contents of the garden. They discuss the seeds that should be ordered (both vegetables and flowers) and when and where these should be planted. Ellen clearly planned ahead and was particularly concerned about securing the supply of vegetables for the following year. She also monitored the progress her neighbours were making in their gardens, at one point begging Ladd to please start digging over the soil 'at once' as 'Mrs Gwynne's gardener has been at it for months and now he too is sowing seeds'.

The letters also explain which flowers Ellen would like planted: lilies, night-scented stocks, roses and, sweet peas (her favourite). The lilies and night-scented stocks were to be planted under windows where she could appreciate them through the summer.

Ellen regularly asks Ladd to ensure baskets of vegetables are sent to London at least once a week. These were to include peas (her favourite vegetable), beans, leeks (only for cooking or for the maids to eat), onions, some potatoes, and spinach. She also requests plenty of herbs, including chives, mint, parsley, sage, tarragon and thyme. The importance Ellen attached to this supply of vegetables and herbs may have stemmed from the spiralling cost of food in London (as compared with that in the countryside), together with the enforcement of compulsory rationing in 1918, which continued in some form into 1920.

Organised chaos

Surviving photographs also provide tantalising glimpses of the garden's layout. They reveal the presence of an orchard (possibly created by Ellen's third husband, James Carew) and a tennis court, which was also used as a croquet lawn.

They also document the presence of many pergolas, one of which still exists towards the top of the garden, in an area that used to be part of the Priest House. It has recently been restored to its original length and planted with 52 roses. Other features from the photographs that can still be seen include the Old Well, also in the former grounds of the Priest House, and the pond, upon which Ellen liked to relax in her boat.

Above right Smallhythe's garden in June

Below right The boat on the Smallhythe pond

Opposite Ellen in the Smallhythe garden

The Garden: family feuds and fun

Slightly more is known about the garden surrounding the adjoining Priest House, which once accounted for half of the garden here. This was fairly wild in places and described by Vita Sackville-West as '[…] like an embroidered cloth spread out on the edge of the Marsh'. As she recalled, it was full of '[…] crab-trees, rounded like giant umbrellas' alongside 'red hot pokers' and 'lilies flanked the pathway'.

There was also a miniature herb garden and, amid the roses, a small tombstone marking the grave of Edy's dog, Ben (1902–13). Vita Sackville-West explained that the inscription on the stone reads 'Dear Dog' because, while the family couldn't honestly describe Ben as 'good', he had certainly been extremely 'dear'.

A family feud

The hedge just to the north of the nuttery was planted by Edy Craig after Ellen married James Carew. Edy did not like Carew and she planted the hedge to ensure that she would never have to see him. The gate between the two houses was also locked while Carew was in residence at Smallhythe.

The white wooden structure that is still present at the top of the garden was once used as a smoking hut by St John (Edy did not permit smoking in the house, but would allow it in the garden and this hut). St John also wrote here.

Right Christopher St John's smoking (and writing) hut

A retreat

Except for the short period of tension during Ellen and Carew's marriage (1907–9), the garden provided a peaceful escape from London and a fun, sociable space. When her grandchildren came to visit in 1909 they played cricket in the ground with their father and Ellen was also willing to join in their games, dressing up in a costume she had once worn as Nance Oldfield in 1909 to entertain her granddaughter Nellie. The cow byre (situated below the side window of the Terry Room) provided a particularly useful space for relaxed tea parties, offering shade in the summer and shelter if it rained.

Opposite, clockwise from top left: Ellen Terry reading in Smallhythe's cow byre, accompanied by a dog; Edward Gordon Craig, his wife Elena Meo, and their children Edward (Little Teddy) and Ellen (Nellie) playing with a dog by the Smallhythe pond; Ellen, Gordon Craig, Elena, Little Teddy and Nellie, in Smallhythe's cow byre, 1910; Ellen in the garden, her grandchild holding up the train of her 'Nance Oldfield' costume; Edy, Tony Atwood and Christopher St John playing croquet on the lawn near the Priest House

DAME ELLEN TERRY
& GRANDCHILD

Smallhythe Village

SMALLHYTHE FERRY.

For at least three hundred years (between the 13th and mid-16th century), long before Ellen Terry moved here, Smallhythe was one of medieval England's most significant shipbuilding centres.

Unlike nearby Rye and Winchelsea, Smallhythe's settlement was not characterised by docks, quaysides and merchant activity and most of the shipbuilding, ship-repairing and ship-breaking activity took place at the river's edge.

Little remains of this medieval shipyard today, beyond traces of boat launches, or slipways, which are just visible as slight depressions in the fields to the east and west of Smallhythe Place. However, it played a significant role in the history of England's shipbuilding.

Smallhythe's port and community

Situated on the broad River Rother, Smallhythe was the port for nearby Tenterden and was listed as a 'limb' of the Cinque Ports from 1449. The Cinque Ports, a number of coastal towns in Kent and Sussex, provided the ships and men who guarded the vulnerable south-east coast from attack from across the Channel. These ports

Above The Smallhythe Ferry in 1900, which took foot passengers across the channel. Smallhythe Place can be seen in the distance

Right Smallhythe Church, with its vicarage on the left (this was destroyed by fire in 1912). The Priest House can be seen to the right

were required to supply 57 ships, each with a crew of 21 men and a boy, for 15 days every year. In return they were granted special rights, including the ability to levy local taxes and exemption from the jurisdiction of certain courts.

Smallhythe's main settlement was centred on the road leading down to the riverbank and on Strand Syde, the road along the north bank of the river; most of the shipbuilding and related activity took place at Strand Syde. The ferry to the Isle of Oxney also departed from here; this provided an important link between the northern and southern Cinque Port towns.

A Royal shipyard

During the 15th century, several wealthy families dominated here, and the majority were involved in shipbuilding. Among them was Sir Robert Brigandyne. Brigandyne, who is believed to have lived and worked in the building now known as the Priest House was a master shipwright. He served both Henry VII and Henry VIII, as Clerk of the King's Ships and oversaw the construction of the *Mary Rose* and another great ship, *Henri Grace a Dieu* (nicknamed 'the Great Harry'), which had its timbers cut at Smallhythe.

This was not the first royal ship to be built at Smallhythe. In 1410, the *Marie*, a 110-ton vessel had been constructed there for Henry IV. Four years later (the year before Agincourt), Henry V came to Smallhythe to inspect the two vessels he had commissioned – the *George*, a balinger of 120 tons and the first British 1,000-ton ship, the *Jesus*.

A century and half later, in 1546, Smallhythe received its last Royal Commission, when Henry VIII ordered the *Great Gallyon* to be built there. At 300 tons, she was both the last of the Great Ships and the last large vessel constructed in Smallhythe.

'No haven there'

By the mid-16th century, several shops and inns had been established at Smallhythe. But although local businesses were still trading, the River Rother had begun to silt up, placing the port under threat. Records of baptisms, marriages and deaths diminish, suggesting a fall in population, and, in 1549, an enquiry was held to establish whether the chapel should be retained. One witness reported: 'There is no haven there, saving only a creeke of salt water where no ship can come buy onely lyters and such kind of small vessels – and that only at full water'.

In 1636, the deliberate breaching of a 300-year-old dam upstream on the River Rother caused the main flow of the river to revert to its former course to the west of Smallhythe. Initially the old stretch of the river continued to provide an important highway for cargo, such as iron and wood, but as it silted up further it became impossible for larger ships to reach Smallhythe. Unable to maintain its status as a port, Smallhythe's shipbuilding industry fell into permanent decline and it became a quiet agricultural area and backwater. The last record of a sailing vessel reaching Smallhythe is from the beginning of the 20th century, at which point the railway finally came to Tenterden.

The buildings at Smallhythe

In 1515, a fire devastated the entire village and port of Smallhythe.

The wooden Chapel was destroyed and subsequently rebuilt in brick. It's likely that Smallhythe Place and the neighbouring Priest House were also constructed around this time.

Smallhythe Place

Little is known about the early history of the main building at Smallhythe Place, which was defined as a 'continuous jetty house' because the upper storage overhangs the lower. The expensive close-studded timber structure has been altered over time, but many original features remain. The Dining Room, for instance, still retains its inglenook fireplace with its 16th-century cast-iron fireback, and marks of a spit machine on the lintel show that this room was once used for cooking.

The original building had two entrances. These were positioned next to one another at the front of the house (bordering the road). One of these was for private use and led to the domestic house. The other led through the hall to what is now the Terry Room, which was decorated with elaborate wall paintings. While it's unlikely that Smallhythe Place was ever the home of the Portreeve (or harbour master), the building is likely to have incorporated a specialised business function within it, possibly in the reception room.

The layout of the building changed after the decline in shipbuilding in the late 16th century. The two wings, which previously extended to the east (forming an open courtyard at the rear), were demolished, and it was converted into a more conventional form to serve as a farmhouse. It was at this point that the present chimneys were constructed, ceilings were added to the upper-floor rooms (previously open to the roof) and one of the two front doorways was blocked.

Further modifications were made to the house in the 19th century, and it was probably during this period that a passageway was added to the first floor to allow private access to each of the four chambers. A stable block and lean-to (serving as a cattle shelter) was added at the south. Above this, and accessed by an external flight of steps, was a small roofed space that served as a fodder loft or tack room. During Ellen Terry's time at Smallhythe, this room was converted into an artist's studio for Tony Atwood (see p. 50). Today it provides a store for the important collection of theatre costumes assembled by Ellen and Edy Craig.

The Priest House

The house between Smallhythe Place and the church can be dated to the same period as Smallhythe Place. In its early years it may have been the home of influential ship builders (see p. 61), but by about 1800 it had been divided to form a pair of unequal cottages. These alterations were reversed in the early 20th century when Ellen purchased the house and presented it to Edy and Christoper St John.

The Barn Theatre

Evidence suggests that from the 15th century, and possibly even earlier, there has been a structure where the Barn Theatre now stands. Several of the timbers in the roof appear to be scorched and even charred, which might suggest that they were salvaged from the 1515 fire (although they might have been damaged by fire after the barn was built). Although the building has experienced multiple modifications since this period, the current roof structure dates from the 17th century and the overall structure of the building was carefully preserved when the Barn was converted into a theatre in the 1920s.

Perhaps the oldest part of the theatre is actually the linenfold panelling that covers half of the back of the acting area. This is said to be '[...] part of the Tudor portion of Hampton Court Palace' which Ellen saw 'on a rubbish tip when visiting a friend in the Grace and Favour apartments'. Hearing that it was surplus to repair work and was going to be burnt, she had it sent to Smallhythe – it was then stored in the barn where it became part of the structure and has since been used in many productions.

Above The Dining Room with its 16th-century fireplace

Right The exterior of Smallhythe and the church

Far right The Smallhythe Barn prior to its conversion

Smallhythe Place and
the garden in June